WOMAN'S OWN BOOK OF

CAKE DECORATING

AND CAKE MAKING

WOMAN'S OWN BOOK OF
CAKE
DECORATING
AND CAKE MAKING

GEORGE NEWNES LIMITED
TOWER HOUSE · SOUTHAMPTON STREET
LONDON, W.C. 2

Printed in Italy by Arnoldo Moudadori – Officine Grafiche – Verona

CONTENTS

The Editor gratefully acknowledges the help of Brown and Polson, the British Sugar Corporation, Cadbury Bros., the Coffee Advisory Board, Colman's Fine Semolina, the Flour Advisory Bureau, Fowler's West India Treacle, Louis Roederer Champagne, McDougalls Cookery Service, Pol Roger Champagne, Stork Cookery Service and Tala.

COLOUR ILLUSTRATIONS

HOW TO MAKE BEAUTIFUL BASIC SPONGE CAKES

A beautifully decorated cake will certainly please the eye, but it will only be a complete success if it tastes as good as it looks. For this reason, the *Woman's Own Book of Cake Decorating and Making* begins with a chapter on the basic types of sponge cake, with charts, hints and recipes to help you make a perfect cake every time. These recipes you can use as a basis for your own decoration ideas. In a later chapter you will find a section on making successful fruit cakes, and throughout the book, many complete recipes for cakes and their decoration.

With such a wealth of tempting recipes to choose from, you will soon be making all kinds of delectable cakes for every occasion – for a wedding or formal party, for a child's birthday tea, or a social evening with friends. Although you will find the simple decorating methods in the earlier part of the book, all the instructions are straightforward and easy to follow. With practice (and this is essential) you will soon be able to carry out the most elaborate designs in piping.

The basic recipes are followed by simple fillings and icings, and many forms of decorating which do not require icing tubes. Methods of preparing and coating cakes for pipe work are carefully described and shown in photographs so that you may see just how it is done. There is a comprehensive chapter on the technique of piping, and another on the fascinating art of making separate sugar decorations by an expert in this field, Mrs Audrey Ellis. Then there are many examples of cakes for important occasions which call for these special skills. The examples chosen are very varied in design, so that by copying details from different cakes, you can build up attractive designs of your own.

Accuracy is essential in measuring ingredients.

Measurement Conversion Chart

British Standard	American Standard
Solids	
1 lb. butter, margarine or other fat	2 cups
1 lb. flour	4 cups

(The term 'self-raising' indicates baking powder has been added.)

1 lb. granulated or castor sugar	2 cups

(Castor sugar is granulated sugar refined to a finer grain.)

1 lb. icing sugar (or confectioner's sugar)	3 cups
1 oz. flour	1 heaped tablespoon
1 oz. sugar	1 level tablespoon
1 oz. butter, margarine or other fat	2 level tablespoons
1 lb. dried fruit	2 cups

Liquids

1 pint equals 20 fl.oz.	1 pint equals 16 fl.oz.
2/5 pint	1 cup

Great care should always be taken to ensure that the temperature of the oven is correct. Here is a chart to help you, but it can only be an approximate guide since cookers vary. But with a little experience you will soon be able to judge whether you need to adjust the temperature given according to the requirements of your particular oven.

Oven Temperature Guide

	ELECTRICITY Fahrenheit deg.	GAS Mark
Very cool	240–265	¼–½
Very slow	290	1
Low	310	2
Very moderate	335	3
Moderate	350	4
Moderately hot	375	5
Hot	400–425	6–7
Very hot	450–475	8–9

Nothing could be more trying than to find that, having made a good cake, you cannot turn it out of the tin without leaving part of the cake behind; or worse still, that you cannot turn it out at all. This can only be avoided by preparing tins with care according to the type of cake to be cooked. Generally speaking, richer cakes, where there is a high proportion of fat to other ingredients, do not tend to stick. But light, sponge-type cakes, particularly fatless sponges (except Angel cakes), stick rather easily. In a later chapter the preparation of tins for fruit cakes is described, but now we are only concerned with making sponges. Here is a useful chart to refer to when getting tins ready for sponge-type cakes.

Preparation of Cake Tins

Bun tins for small cakes should be lightly greased with clarified fat, or the fat used in making the cakes.

Swiss roll tins should be lined with a piece of greaseproof paper large enough to cover base and sides of tin. Lightly grease paper, making sure it is pressed well into the corners of the tin.

Round sandwich tins should be greased and dusted with equal quantities of flour and sugar mixed.

This gives a crisp finish to the outside of the cake. If liked, line bottom first with greaseproof paper.

Funnel tins for Angel cake should not be greased, but the cake must be allowed to stand in the inverted tin for 30 minutes after removing from the oven, before being turned out on a cooling tray.

Deep round, loaf or square tins for plain cakes should be prepared as for round sandwich tins.

SWISS ROLL

You require: 3 large eggs • 3 oz. castor sugar • 3 oz. self-raising flour • 4 level tbsp. warmed jam •

Grease and line Swiss roll tin, 9 in. × 12 in. Take eggs at room temperature and whisk with sugar until the mixture is light and creamy and the whisk leaves a trail when lifted out of the mixture. Fold in sifted flour using a metal spoon. Turn into prepared tin and smooth level with a palette knife. Bake in a hot oven at Mark 7, 425 deg., until sponge begins to shrink from the edges of the tin and is pale golden brown, about 7-10 minutes. Turn on to a sheet of greaseproof paper dredged with castor sugar. Trim edges of sponge, spread with jam and roll up tightly. Dredge with castor sugar and cool.
Note: For a smaller Swiss roll baked in a 7 in.× 11 in. tin use: 2 large eggs, 2 oz. castor sugar, 2 oz. self-raising flour, 3 level tbsp. warmed jam.

VICTORIA SANDWICH
Colour plate one

You require: For sponge: 4 oz. self-raising flour • pinch salt • 4 oz. butter or margarine, or mixture of both • 4 oz. castor sugar • 2 standard eggs • For filling: approx. 2 level tbsp. raspberry jam •

Sift flour and salt. Cream fat and sugar till light and fluffy, then beat in eggs, one at a time. Fold in dry ingredients with a metal spoon, then divide mixture equally between 2 well-greased 6-7 in. sandwich tins. Bake in the centre of the oven at Mark 4, 350 deg., for 25-30 minutes. Turn out and cool on a wire tray. Fill with jam and dust with castor sugar. For chocolate flavour, add ½ oz. sieved cocoa and 1 dessertspoon black treacle to dry ingredients.

Swiss Roll

Victoria Sandwich

Quantities of mixture for larger sandwich cakes

For two 7-8 in. tins or one deeper tin use:

6 oz. self-raising or plain flour with 1½ level
  teasp. of baking powder
6 oz. butter
6 oz. sugar
3 eggs

For two 8-9 in. tins or one deeper tin use:

8 oz. self-raising or plain flour with 2 level
  teasp. of baking powder
8 oz. butter
8 oz. sugar
4 eggs

Cream butter and sugar until well-blended. Beat the eggs and gradually add to the creamed butter. Now fold in the sieved flour using a metal spoon to avoid over-beating. Put the mixture into greased tins. Set oven at Mark 4-5, 350-375 deg., and bake just above centre for 25-30 minutes for the 7-8 in. tins, and 30-35 minutes for the 8-9 in. tins. One deep tin should be baked in the centre of the oven at Mark 3, 335 deg. 50 minutes for a 7-8 in. tin; 60 minutes for a 8-9 in. tin.

CHOCOLATE LAYER CAKE

You require: 4 oz. butter • 5 oz. castor sugar •
3 eggs • little vanilla essence • 6 oz. plain flour •
1 oz. cocoa • 3 level teasp. baking powder •

Cream butter and sugar until light and fluffy. Beat in eggs one at a time. Add dash of vanilla. Sift together flour, cocoa and baking powder, fold into creamed mixture, adding a tablespoon of milk if needed to make a thick dropping consistency. Bake in 2 greased 8 in. tins, in a moderate oven, Mark 5, 375 deg., for about 25 minutes. Cool on a wire tray.

When cakes are cold, sandwich together with chocolate butter cream filling (see page 21). Decorate top with sieved icing sugar.

For a specially attactive finish, place a paper doiley on top of the cake, then dust liberally with icing sugar. Lift doiley with extreme care so as not to smudge the pattern. (See picture on page 21.)

The finished chocolate layer cake made from the three stages shown opposite

Coffee sponge sandwich

Make a basic Victoria sandwich mixture and add 1 teaspoon of instant coffee powder to each 2 oz. flour. Follow baking instructions of plain sponge.

Making coffee sponge sandwich by the whisking method

This is the method to use for a light sponge cake. Whisk together 3 large eggs and 4 oz. castor sugar in a large basin until thick and creamy. Some people like to whisk over a saucepan of hot, but not boiling, water, but others believe that you get a lighter consistency without using heat. If you are whisking over heat, whisk until thick and creamy, remove from heat and whisk until mixture is cool. The mixture should be sufficiently thick to see the trail of the whisk for some seconds. Sieve 3 oz. plain flour thoroughly, twice if possible. Then fold into the eggs and sugar very

carefully with a metal spoon or palette knife. Now fold in 1 tablespoon of hot, but not boiling, water. Grease and flour one 8 in. or two 7 in. baking tins. Pour mixture into the cake tins. Bake 8 in. cake in the centre of the oven at Mark 5, 375 deg. for about 25 minutes, or Mark 2, 310 deg., for about 45 minutes. Bake 7 in. cake above centre of oven for 9-10 minutes at Mark 6-7, 400-425 deg., or at Mark 4, 350 deg. for 14-15 minutes. Cool before turning out.

Only plain flour is given in the recipe and this is quite correct, for so much air is incorporated by whisking the eggs, etc. that the cake will be light. Only a small proportion of flour to eggs is given in this type of recipe and high proportion of sugar. Do not cut down on this for it plays a part in making the sponge light. Time the baking carefully as this is a very delicate sponge mixture and is easily dried and overcooked.

SPONGE FLAN

You require: For flan: 4 oz. super sifted self-raising flour • pinch salt • 4 oz. butter or margarine • 4 oz. castor sugar • 2 eggs • For filling: small cans cherries, peaches and pears • 2 bananas • ¼ lb. black grapes • ½ pkt. lemon jelly • just under ½ pint syrup from the cans •

Brush an 8 in. round sponge flan tin with melted lard or vegetable cooking fat. Sieve the flour and salt. Beat the fat until soft, add the sugar and beat again until light in colour and fluffy in texture. Add the eggs one at a time, together with a tablespoon of flour with each egg, beating well after each addition. Stir in the rest of the flour. Spread mixture evenly in the tin, bake at Mark 5, 375 deg., for 20-25 minutes.
Make filling: Drain fruits, dissolve jelly in enough hot syrup to make up to ½ pint. Put away in a cool place until cold and just starting to thicken. Meanwhile place the flan on a serving plate. Stone the grapes, slice the bananas, peaches and pears and fill the flan with the fruit. When jelly begins to thicken, pour over the fruit and leave to set.

CHOCOLATE SPONGE FLAN

You require: For sponge: 2 eggs • 2 oz. castor sugar • 2 oz. self-raising flour • 1 dessp. cocoa • For filling: ½ pkt. jelly • ¼ pint boiling water • ¼ pint evaporated milk • glacé cherries •

Whisk eggs and sugar until thick and fluffy. Fold in the sieved flour and cocoa. Pour into a well-greased 8 in. flan tin. Bake at Mark 5, 375 deg., for about 15-20 minutes. Cool on a wire tray. Make filling: Dissolve the jelly in the boiling water. Allow to cool and thicken slightly. Add the evaporated milk and whisk until the mixture is light and fluffy. Pour into the flan case. Put into a cool place until firm. Decorate with glacé cherries.

ANGEL CAKE

You require: 4 oz. flour • 6 oz. castor sugar • 6 eggs whites • ½ level teasp. cream of tartar • ½ teasp. vanilla essence and a few drops almond essence for flavouring •

Sieve flour and sugar into separate bowls. Whisk egg whites until very stiff and then fold in sieved cream of tartar. Fold half sugar into egg whites, then sieved flour, flavourings and finally rest of sugar. Put into an ungreased, deep 8 in. ring tin or 7 in. cake tin. To remove air bubbles, draw a knife through mixture several times. Bake 1 hour at Mark 3, 335 deg., in the ring tin, 1¼ hours in the cake tin. Turn the tin upside-down on a cake tray and leave until tin and cake are cold – the cake will then fall out whole.
Angel Cake is especially delicious filled with pink frosting, accompanied by strawberry ice cream or coated with pink frosting and decorated with melted plain chocolate.

LEMON CHIFFON CAKE

You require: 4 oz. self-raising flour • 5 oz. castor sugar • ½ level teasp. salt • 4 tbsp. corn oil • 3 egg yolks • 5 tbsp. water • ½ teasp. vanilla essence • finely grated rind of half a lemon • ½ level teasp. of cream of tartar • 3 egg whites •

Sift flour, sugar and salt together three times. Make a well in the centre and add, in this order, the oil, egg yolks, water, vanilla essence and lemon rind. Stir briskly until batter is smooth. Sprinkle cream of tartar over the egg whites and beat until very stiff, stiffer than necessary for meringues. (It is essential that the egg whites be at room temperature before beating.) Pour batter on to the egg whites, a third at a time, then fold in very gently, preferably with a rubber spatula or, if unavailable, with a metal spoon. Take care not to stir the mixture. Pour into a 7-8 in. sloping-sided, ungreased tube tin and bake in the centre of a moderate oven, Mark 3, 335 deg., for about 1 hour.
Invert the tin over a large funnel or bottle and leave to 'hang' till thoroughly cool, about 1 hour. To remove cake, loosen edges with a knife and tap the base of the tin sharply, it should then come out easily.

Tested tips

1. The mixture may curdle when the eggs are added to the creamed butter and sugar. If this happens, quickly add a little flour.

Chocolate Sponge Flan

Lemon Chiffon Cake

2. Spread the Victoria sponge mixture away from the centre of the tin. This will ensure that the sponge will be flat when it has been cooked.

3. It is important that sponge mixtures should be cooked for exactly the right length of time, as even a few minutes over-cooking tends to make them dry and leathery. If the sponge feels resilient and springs back after the light pressure of a finger tip, it is sufficiently cooked.

4. Take care in turning out the sponge. First, loosen by tapping the tin on the table with a firm movement. Now gently rest your hand on top of the sponge and carefully turn it upside down, removing the tin. Ease on to a wire cooling tray.

FEATHER SPONGE

You require: For cake: 5 oz. plain flour • 1 oz. corn-flour • 2 level teasp. baking powder • ½ teasp. salt • 5 oz. castor sugar • 2 eggs • 3½ fl. oz. corn oil • 3½ fl. oz. water • For filling: chocolate butter cream • For decoration: white and chocolate glacé icing •

Line the bases of two 7 in. sandwich tins with greaseproof paper and grease lightly. Sieve the dry ingredients into a bowl. Separate the yolks from the whites of the eggs. Mix together lightly with a fork, the egg yolks, corn oil and water, and stir into the dry ingredients. Beat well to form a smooth, slack batter. Whisk the egg whites stiffly, and fold lightly into the mixture. Turn mixture into prepared tins. Bake at Mark 5, 375 deg., for 25-30 minutes. Remove cakes from tins and cool on a wire tray. Sandwich the cakes together with chocolate butter cream. Cover the top of the cake with white glacé icing. Pipe four rings of chocolate glacé icing on top of the white icing, and while icing is still wet use a skewer to draw eight lines from the centre of the cake to the edge and eight lines from the edge of the cake to the centre, arranging the lines alternately.

Step-by-step stages of making a perfect feather sponge

Plain and Chocolate Victoria Sandwiches

Iced Genoese Sponge

GLACE ICING
BUTTER CREAM
AND
SIMPLE FINISHES

The simplest of all icings is glacé icing because it is so quick and easy to make. It can be flavoured, tinted various shades, and requires no cooking; but liquid should be added warm, not cold. It is ideal for covering every sort of sponge, especially Genoese sponge for large or small fancy cakes.

ICED GENOESE SPONGE
Colour plate two

You require: For sponge: 4 oz. super sifted self-raising flour • pinch salt • 4 oz. castor sugar • 3 eggs • 2 oz. melted butter, unsalted if possible • For glacé icing: 8 oz. icing sugar, sieved • good squeeze of lemon juice • 2-2½ tbsp. warm water • a few drops pink colouring •

Grease an 8 in. round cake tin, cut a circle of greaseproof paper to fit the base, put it in position and grease it lightly. Have ready a large saucepan with 2-3 in. of water in it and a mixing bowl which fits over the pan without touching the water. Bring water to the boil and turn off the heat. Break the eggs into the bowl, add the sugar and whisk over the water for about 5 minutes, until the mixture thickens and is lukewarm. Care must be taken to avoid overheating; the base of the bowl should not feel uncomfortably hot to the hands. Remove the bowl from the pan, place it on the table and continue whisking for another 5 minutes. Pour in the warm melted fat, add the sieved flour and salt. Using a metal spoon cut and fold the flour and fat into the mixture by taking the spoon down across the centre of the mixture, up the side of the basin and over

the centre. Do this very lightly until well mixed. Pour the mixture into the tin and bake, Mark 4, 350 deg., for 35-40 minutes until firm to the touch.

Make glacé icing: Put the sugar into a saucepan, add lemon juice. Add water cautiously and mix to a coating consistency. Add colouring, beat well and stir over gentle heat for 1 minute. Pour over cake.

Flavourings for Glacé Icing

Almond: Add a few drops of almond essence to taste. You can also add cochineal to colour pink.

Chocolate: Put 2 oz. plain chocolate, broken up, into a basin with 1 tablespoon milk and 1 tablespoon water. Melt over hot water, add 4 oz. sieved icing sugar and beat well.

Mocha: Sieve 1 rounded dessertspoon cocoa with 8 oz. icing sugar, mix with strong coffee to spreading consistency. Stir in a teaspoon of melted butter.

Coffee: Mix with strong coffee instead of water.

Lemon: Mix with lemon juice or lemon squash instead of water, and tint with saffron yellow colouring.

Orange: Mix with orange juice plus 1 teaspoon of lemon juice, or orange squash instead of water. If liked, tint with orange food colouring.

Christmas Ring Cake

Of course, many other variations of flavoured glacé icings are given throughout this book, so use these for reference if you are experimenting. By gradually adding the liquid hot, you will get a glossier result than if you use cold liquid.

CHRISTMAS RING CAKE

You require: For cake: 6 oz. butter • 6 oz. castor sugar • 2 whole eggs • 2 extra yolks of eggs • 2 brimming dessp. rum • 1 teasp. grated outer rind of lemon • 2 tbsp. water • 4 tbsp. evaporated milk • 10 oz. self-raising flour, sifted • For decoration: little white glacé icing, vanilla flavoured • angelica cut into small star shapes •

Soften butter and beat well. Add sugar and beat together thoroughly. Separate whole eggs. Whisk whites first, then add yolks and whisk together well. Add gradually with lemon rind to butter and sugar mixture, beating constantly until light and creamy.

If this mixture shows signs of curdling, sift in a teaspoon or so of flour between additions of liquid. Stir in gradually the rum and evaporated milk diluted with the water. When smoothly blended, stir in sifted flour without in any way beating the mixture, which should be of a consistency that will drop from the spoon with a slight shake. Put into a ring tin, previously greased and coated with castor sugar, filling it about three-quarters full. Bake at Mark 4, 350 deg., for about 40 minutes, or until firm to the touch. Cool on a wire tray. Spread cake with glacé icing and decorate with stars made from angelica.

FROSTED FRUIT ROLL

You require: For cake: 4 oz. plain flour • 1 level teasp. baking powder • 2 oz. castor sugar • 2 eggs • 1 tbsp. hot water • 2 tbsp. warm jam • For glacé icing: 8 oz. sieved icing sugar • 2-3 dessp. lemon juice, strained • To decorate: crystallized fruits •

Sieve together the flour and the baking powder. Whisk the eggs and sugar over a basin of hot water until the mixture is thick, white, and will hold its own weight. Add the hot water, then lightly fold in the sieved flour. Spread the mixture into a greaseproof-paper lined tin, 9 in. × 12 in., and bake at Mark 6, 400 deg., for 8-12 minutes. Turn out on to greaseproof paper lightly dusted with castor sugar. Spread immediately with the warmed jam, trim away crisp edge and roll up firmly.

Make glacé icing: Mix together the sugar and lemon juice to form an icing of thick pouring consistency. When cake is cold, pour over the icing and when half set, decorate with crystallized fruit.

CHERRY LAYER CAKE
Colour plate three

You require: For cake: 4 oz. butter • 5 oz. castor sugar • yolks only of 6 eggs or the whole of 3 eggs • 6 oz. self-raising flour • 3 oz. finely chopped cherries • For filling and decoration: butter icing mixed with finely chopped cherries • white glacé icing • cherries • angelica •

Cream together the sugar and butter until very soft. Gradually beat in the egg yolks. When all the eggs have been added, stir in the flour gently and then the finely chopped cherries. Divide the mixture between two 7 in. greased and floured sandwich tins and bake at Mark 5, 375 deg., until golden brown, approximately 25 minutes. Sandwich together with butter and cherry icing, top with glacé icing and decorate with flowers made of cherries and angelica.

LEMON CHERRY LAYER
Colour plates four and five

You require: 12 oz. margarine or butter • 12 oz. castor sugar • 6 eggs • finely grated rind 2 large lemons • 12 oz. self-raising flour • ½ teasp. salt • For the filling: 6 oz. butter • 12 oz. icing sugar • lemon juice • 6 oz.

Frosted Fruit Roll

chopped glacé cherries • For glacé icing topping: 2 oz chopped glacé cherries • 8 oz. icing sugar • warm water •

Grease and line the base of four 9 in. sandwich cake tins. Cream fat and sugar until light and fluffy and beat in eggs one at a time. Add lemon rind. Sift flour and salt, fold in one-third at a time. Divide the mixture equally between the tins, and bake Mark 4, 350 deg. 25-30 minutes. Turn out.

For filling, cream butter, mix in sieved icing sugar and enough lemon juice to give a spreading consistency and a good flavour. Add cherries, use to sandwich layers.

Make topping by mixing cherries and icing sugar with warm water to give a coating consistency. Ice cake. Decorate with more cherries.

Tested tip

For a professional finish, before using glacé icing brush the top and sides of the cake with a pastry brush to remove surplus crumbs. Next brush the cake with a little egg white, allow to dry, then go ahead and ice your cake.

FEATHERED MOCHA BISCUITS

You require: For biscuits: 4 oz. plain flour • 1 teasp. cocoa • pinch salt • 2 oz. margarine or butter • 2 oz. castor sugar • 2 teasp. coffee essence • 1 egg yolk • For icing: icing sugar • coffee essence •

Sieve the flour, cocoa and salt into a bowl. Rub in the fat until the mixture resembles breadcrumbs, and add the castor sugar. Stir in the coffee, with the egg yolk, mixing to a stiff paste. Knead and roll out on a floured board to $\frac{1}{2}$ in. thick. Cut into shapes. Bake on a greased tray at Mark 5, 375 deg., for 10-15 minutes. Cool on a wire tray. Store in a tin and decorate as required. Make icing: Prepare a stiff glacé icing with icing sugar and a little water. Divide into two and flavour half with coffee essence. Place the coffee icing into a greaseproof paper piping bag and cut off the tip. Spread about 1 teasp. white icing on to a biscuit. Immediately pipe on to this straight lines of coffee icing. While still wet, use a fine skewer to draw straight lines at right angles to the coffee lines. Repeat in the opposite direction. Decorate each biscuit before starting on the next. Another type of feathering is the Spider's Web design which is shown as a decoration on the Feather Sponge on page 16. As a variation, spread the biscuits with coffee icing and feather in this design with white icing.

The other most popular type of icing is butter cream or butter icing. This has the added advan-

Feather iced biscuits taste as good as they look and yet they are simplicity itself to ice in this way

tage of being useful as a filling between layers, yet it can (if brought to the right consistency) be used for piping. Basically, this cream is very simply made by beating butter, or good quality margarine, or a white vegetable fat, with icing sugar until a smooth cream results. If you have the time, it will have a more velvety texture if you beat the fat well before adding the sugar. Allow 3-4 oz. fat to 8 oz. icing sugar for a simple cream to fill a 7 in. layer cake. Add 3 dessertspoons of milk with any desired colouring or flavouring to the same quantity of the basic mixture, to make a butter icing to cover and pipe this cake.

Approximately 1 lb. icing sugar and 6-8 oz. fat are required to fill, cover and decorate generously.

Variations for flavouring Butter Cream and Butter Icing

Chocolate: Cream together 4 oz. butter and 8 oz. icing sugar, add a little milk to give a soft, creamy consistency. Blend 1 level tablespoon of cocoa with a little water. Beat in sufficient of this mixture to give colour and flavour you require.

Coffee: Make up the basic mixture and flavour with 1 dessertspoon of coffee essence, or one teaspoon powdered coffee dissolved in a dessertspoon of water.

Vanilla: Add 1 teaspoon vanilla essence to the 3 dessertspoons of milk before blending with the creamed fat and sugar. It can be tinted pink or yellow.

Peppermint: Add 1 teaspoon oil of peppermint to the milk before blending with the creamed fat and sugar. This can be tinted pale green.

Rum: Add a few drops of rum essence or 1 tablespoon of rum to the milk before blending with the creamed fat and sugar. Tint with a few drops of gravy browning.

A very good use for butter icing is to mask the sides of a layer cake, which often do not look neat, and then to roll the sides in chopped nuts or desiccated coconut. Do not coat the top or attempt to decorate it until the sides have been completely covered. Another advantage to using butter icing is that it keeps better than fresh whipped cream. However, the colour is different, so remember when planning a colour scheme and

Lazy Daisy Cake: to decorate, place doiley on top of the cake, dust with icing sugar, then remove doiley

tinting the icing that the stronger shade of yellow the fat used, the more it will affect the colour. For instance, pinks will tend to be more apricot.

ALL-THINGS-NICE CAKE

You require: For cake: 4 oz. butter or margarine • 4 oz. castor sugar • 2 eggs • 2 oz. tenderized coconut • 6 oz. self-raising flour, sieved • 2 tbsp. milk • For cinnamon cream: 6 oz. icing sugar, sieved • 1 rounded teasp. cinnamon • 3 oz. butter or margarine • 1 dessp. milk •

Cream butter or margarine and sugar till light and fluffy, then add the eggs, one at a time, beating thoroughly after each addition. Add coconut, then lightly fold in flour alternately with the milk. Transfer mixture to a well-greased and floured 7 in. plain or fancy cake tin and bake at Mark 3, 335 deg., for 1 to 1¼ hours. Cool on a wire tray. When cold, slice into three layers and sandwich together with cinnamon cream.

Make cinnamon cream by creaming icing sugar and cinnamon with the butter or margarine till

light and fluffy. Beat in the milk. Dust top of the cake with sieved icing sugar. For an interesting effect, place a wire cooling tray over the top of the cake and sprinkle generously with sieved icing sugar. Remove cooling tray.

COFFEE CREAM SPONGE CAKE
Colour plate six

You require: 3 eggs • 1¼ oz. sugar • 6 saccharine tablets • 4 oz. flour, with plain flour use 1 level teasp. baking powder • few drops of vanilla essence • 2 tbsp. hot milk or water • For low-calorie butter filling: 2 oz. butter • 2 tbsp. sugar substitute or about 9 saccharine tablets crushed to a fine powder • 4 oz. cottage cheese • 1 good teasp. instant coffee • 1 tbsp. milk •

Separate the egg whites and the yolks. Whisk the whites until stiff, then whisk the yolks and sugar until creamy and fold in the whites. Dissolve the saccharines in the hot milk or water, mix with the vanilla essence. Carefully fold the flour into the eggs, then add the saccharine liquid and blend in gently. Grease and flour two 7 in. sandwich tins.

All-things-nice Cake

Apricot Ribbon Cake

Pour in mixture, bake in a moderately hot oven, Mark 5, 375 deg. until cooked and golden brown on top, about 18-20 minutes. Turn out and allow to cool before filling with butter cream.

Make low-calorie butter filling: Soften the butter very slightly so that it creams well with the sugar substitute or crushed saccharines. Add the cheese together with the coffee dissolved in the warm milk. Cream very lightly; overcreaming accentuates the pieces of cottage cheese and you do not get as smooth a mixture. Use just under half for the filling, and pile the rest on top of the cake, sweeping it up in points.

APRICOT RIBBON CAKE

You require: 6 eggs • 6 oz. castor sugar • 6 oz. flour • pinch salt • 1 tbsp. warm water • ½-¾ lb. apricot jam or marmalade • For butter icing: 3 oz. butter • 8 oz. icing sugar • 3 dessp. milk • finely grated rind 1 orange • orange food colouring •

Prepare two 8 in. sandwich tins and a 14 in. × 10 in. Swiss roll tin. Make sponge by beating eggs with sugar until thick and creamy. Fold in sifted flour and salt, and then water. Put half mixture into Swiss roll tin and divide rest between sandwich tins. Bake at Mark 7, 425 deg. for 10-15 minutes. Turn oblong cake out on to

sugared paper, trim ends and roll up inside paper. Leave to cool. Turn other two cakes on to a wire tray. Unroll cake, spread with jam and cut into six strips 1½ in. wide. Roll up one strip like a Swiss roll and place cut side down on a plate, roll remaining strips round it like a large pinwheel. Place one round cake on a plate and spread with jam. Carefully slide the 'pinwheel' on top, spread with jam. Put top layer of cake on.

For icing, beat butter and sugar together until creamy, add milk and orange rind, beat again, add colouring as desired. Use to cover cake, roughing up into points with a knife.

Tested tips

1. Butter icing sometimes breaks the sponge when it is spread on it. If this happens, add a tiny amount of water or milk to soften the icing slightly.

2. If your butter icing looks rather sticky and a little greasy, add some more icing sugar.

3. To get butter icing to the right consistency it must be creamed. Never be tempted to take the short cut of warming the butter first to soften it, this only results in an oily cream. However, you can use a warm knife if this is helpful in spreading.

HAZEL NUT GATEAU

You require: For cake: 6 oz. margarine or butter • 6 oz. castor sugar • 3 eggs • 6 oz. self-raising flour • 2 teasp. cocoa • For filling: glacé or canned cherries • butter cream • chopped hazel nuts • For decoration: butter cream • crushed cornflakes • hazel nuts • marzipan cherries •

Grease and line three 7 in. sponge tins. Cream the fat and sugar until light and fluffy. Beat in the eggs. Fold in the sieved flour adding sufficient warm water to form a soft dropping consistency. Take two-thirds of the mixture and divide into two of the tins. To the remaining mixture add the sieved cocoa and a little more warm water to keep the required consistency. Spread evenly into the other sponge tin. Bake at Mark 5, 375 deg., for about 20-25 minutes.

Make filling: Chop the hazel nuts, leaving 12 whole for decoration. Cut the cherries into small pieces. Add both to the butter cream. Use this filling to sandwich together the three sponge layers placing the chocolate one in the centre.

Hazel Nut Gâteau

To decorate, spread butter cream evenly around the sides. Dip into crushed cornflakes. Spread the remaining butter cream over the top. Use a hot, flat knife to obtain a smooth result. Decorate with whole hazel nuts and marzipan cherries.

CARIBBEAN CAKE

You require: For cake: 6 oz. butter or margarine • 6 oz. castor sugar • 6 level tbsp. black treacle • 2 standard eggs • 1 oz. cocoa powder • 1 oz. cornflour • 6 oz. self-raising flour • 5 tbsp. milk • For rum butter cream: 8 oz. butter • 12 oz. icing sugar, sifted • 2 level tbsp. black treacle • 6 tbsp. cold milk • 2 tbsp. rum • 4 tbsp. boiling water •

Cream butter, sugar and black treacle till light and fluffy. Add eggs, one at a time, beating well after each. Sift together cocoa powder, cornflour and flour and turn into creamed mixture alternately with the milk. Turn into 2 greased and paper-lined 7 in. sandwich tins and bake in the centre of a moderate oven, Mark 4, 350 deg., for 30-35 minutes. Turn out and cool on a wire tray.

*Cherry Layer Cake
and Golden Fruit Cake*

Lemon Cherry Layer

Coffee Cream Sponge Cake

Coffee Fudge Chocolate Cake

Caribbean Cake

When cold, cut in half then sandwich together and coat top and sides with rum butter cream. Make rum butter cream: Cream butter, sugar and black treacle well together. Beat in milk and rum gradually. Whisk in water, a tablespoon at a time.

DOBOS TORTE

You require: 6 eggs • 6 oz. castor sugar • 6 oz. plain flour • pinch salt • 2 tbsp. warm water • For caramel: 4 oz. sugar • 2½ fl. oz. water • For filling: 4 oz. plain chocolate • 6 oz. butter • 1 lb. sieved icing sugar • warm water • For decoration: nuts •

Grease and flour 3 baking sheets for each half quantity. Mark a 7 in. round on each sheet. Make up sponge, using half the quantities, put eggs and sugar into bowl. Whisk until mixture will hold impression of whisk for few seconds. Fold in sifted flour and salt, then the warm water. Divide mixture in three and spread carefully over rounds marked on baking sheets. Bake at Mark 8, 450 deg., for 8-10 minutes. When cold trim edges. Repeat using rest of cake ingredients, making 6

layers in all. Place one layer on wire rack for caramel topping.

Make caramel: put sugar and water in pan. Stir over low heat until sugar dissolves. Raise heat and boil until mixture turns a caramel colour. Pour over cake layer so top is evenly coated. Quickly mark into sections using back of oiled knife.

Make filling: break chocolate into small pieces and melt in basin over pan of hot water. Allow to cool but not harden. Cream butter, stir in icing sugar, then beat until well mixed. Stir in chocolate and enough warm water to give a spreading consistency. Use some to sandwich cake layers together. Put caramel covered layer on top. Spread rest of butter cream round sides, then coat with nuts. These should be hazel nuts, but could be a mixture of hazel nuts, almonds, walnuts, unsalted peanuts, or any one of these varieties. They should be roughly chopped. Stand the cake on a sheet of greaseproof paper and press the nuts lightly against the sides until evenly coated.

GATEAU LOUISE

You require: For sauce: 8 oz. plain chocolate • 3½ oz. castor sugar • ¼ pint water • 1½ teasp. instant coffee • 2 teasp. vanilla essence • For the pastry: 8 oz. plain flour • 2 oz. cornflour • pinch of salt • 5 oz. butter • ½ pint double cream • a little rum or Cointreau • grated chocolate •

Make the sauce. Put the chocolate, sugar, water and instant coffee into a saucepan and melt together very slowly until the sauce is smooth, stir in the vanilla essence. Divide in half and leave to cool.

To make the pastry, sieve together the dry ingredients and rub in the butter. Stir in half the chocolate sauce and beat the mixture until well blended and smooth. Divide mixture in half and spread one-third of this amount over the bottom of each of three inverted 8 in. tins. Bake at Mark 6, 400 deg., for 5-8 minutes. Repeat with rest of mixture, making 6 layers altogether.

Whip the cream until thick and stir in the remaining chocolate sauce with the rum or Cointreau to taste. Sandwich together the layers of cake with the cream, reserving sufficient to decorate the top. Sprinkle with grated chocolate. Chill before serving.

LEMON BUTTER CAKE

You require: 4 oz. butter • 4 oz. castor sugar • 2 eggs • finely grated rind of 1 lemon • 4 oz. self-raising flour • pinch salt • For filling: 3-4 tbsp. lemon curd • For topping: 2 oz. butter • 6 oz. sieved icing sugar • lemon juice •

Grease two 7 in. sandwich tins and line base with greaseproof paper. Cream butter and sugar and beat in eggs one at a time. Add the lemon rind and fold in the self-raising flour sieved with the salt. Divide between the two sandwich cake tins and bake for 20-25 minutes at Mark 3, 335 deg. When cool, sandwich together with the lemon curd. Make the topping by creaming the butter and stirring in the sieved icing sugar with sufficient lemon juice to give a spreading consistency. Spread over the top and mark in swirls with the tip of a palette knife, or mark with a fork.

Gâteau Louise

Four simple stages to making a chocolate Swiss roll. Decorate it as a Yule log or child's birthday log

CHOCOLATE SWISS ROLL

You require: 3 eggs • 3 oz. castor sugar • 2½ oz. self-raising flour • 1 level tbsp. cocoa • fresh whipped cream •

Whisk the eggs and the sugar until thick, light and fluffy. Carefully fold in the sieved flour and cocoa. Pour into a greased and lined Swiss roll tin approximately 12 in. × 9 in. Bake in oven Mark 6, 400 deg., for 10-15 minutes. Turn at once on to a piece of sugared greaseproof paper. Trim the edge of the sponge using a sharp knife, and carefully roll it up so that the greaseproof paper is inside. Allow to cool and then gently unroll. Remove the paper. Spread sponge evenly with cream and re-roll, taking care not to crack it.

To finish the cake, sift with icing sugar through a coarse sieve if required as a Yule Log, and add such ornaments as a holly spray or china robin.

Birthday Chocolate Log: Do not sift with icing sugar, but arrange a trail of sugar flowers over the top and sides of the cake, allowing room for the number of candles required. Insert candles into the icing, chilling the cake slightly first so that the icing is firm and will support them upright. The photograph on the right gives a good guide.

27

HONEY ALMOND DESSERT CAKE

You require: For cake: 4 oz. butter or margarine •
2 oz. soft brown sugar • 2 level tbsp. thick honey •
2 standard eggs • 6 oz. self-raising flour, sieved •
4 tbsp. milk • For topping and filling: 3 oz. butter •
1 rounded tbsp. thick honey • 3 oz. icing sugar, sieved
• 1½ oz. flaked toasted almonds •

Grease and line a deep 7 in. round cake tin.
Cream butter, sugar and honey together until
light and fluffy. Beat in blended eggs thoroughly,
adding a little of the flour with the last amount
of egg. Fold in remaining flour and milk. Turn
into prepared tin and bake at Mark 4, 350 deg.,
for 45 minutes. Turn out and cool on a wire
tray.
Make topping and filling: Soften butter and beat
in honey and icing sugar. Cut cake in half and
fill with half the butter cream. Put together again
and cover top and sides with butter cream. Scatter
with flaked almonds.

CHOCOLATE CHIFFON TORTE

You require: For cake: 4 level tbsp. cocoa • 8 tbsp
boiling water • 7 oz. castor sugar • 3 oz. flour • 2
teasp. baking powder • pinch salt • 4 eggs • 3 oz.
butter, melted • ¼ teasp. cream of tartar • vanilla essence • For butter cream: 3 oz. butter • 6 oz. icing
sugar • 1 level teasp. cocoa dissolved in 1 tbsp. hot
water • For decoration: 6 milk flake bars •

Blend the cocoa with the boiling water and leave
to cool. Sieve the sugar, flour, baking powder
and salt into a bowl and beat in the egg yolks and
melted butter. Add the cocoa mixture and vanilla
essence and beat until smooth. Whisk the egg
whites with the cream of tartar, until stiff, and
fold into the chocolate mixture. Pour into an ungreased 8 in. cake tin. Bake at Mark 4, 350 deg.,
for about 45-55 minutes. Invert immediately on
to a cake rack but do not turn out until cold.
Make the butter cream by creaming the butter
and icing sugar together and add cocoa. Spread
some cream round the outside of the cake and
roll in two of the flake bars, crumbled. Decorate
the top with butter cream, and remaining flake
bars, halved.

APRICOT AMARETTI SPONGE

You require: For cake: 6 oz. butter or margarine •
6 oz. castor sugar • 3 eggs • 2 oz. ground almonds •
6 oz. self-raising flour, sifted • For almond cream:
12 oz. icing sugar, sieved • 6 oz. butter or margarine,
slightly softened • 2 tbsp. milk, or brandy or sherry •
few drops almond essence • For topping: 3 oz. ratafias (tiny almond macaroons) • 1 large can apricot
halves, drained of syrup • 1-2 tbsp. apricot jam, melted
and sieved •

Cream fat and sugar together till light and fluffy.
Beat in eggs, one at a time, adding a level table-

Honey Almond Dessert Cake

Apricot Amaretti Sponge

spoon of flour with each to prevent curdling. Add almonds, then lightly fold in flour with a metal spoon. Divided mixture equally between two well-greased 8 in. sandwich tins and bake towards the top of a moderately hot oven, Mark 5, 375 deg., for 25-30 minutes, till well risen, firm and golden. Cool on wire tray.

Cream icing sugar and fat together till fluffy and light; beat in milk, or brandy or sherry, and essence. Sandwich cake together with a thick layer of cream, then spread remainder over top and sides. Press ratafias in rows against sides of cake. Cover top with the drained apricot halves, cut sides down. Glaze by brushing with a little warmed apricot jam. Chill before serving.

Variations of Chocolate Layer Cake
(see basic recipe on page 12)

Chocolate Apple Cake: Use Basic Recipe. Omit milk and vanilla. Melt chocolate in 3 tablespoons water. Add ¼ pint unsweetened, stewed apple. When sifting flour and salt, add 1 level teaspoon baking powder and ½ level teaspoon mixed spice or cinnamon to the mixture.

Mocha Cake: Use Basic Recipe. Omit milk and melt chocolate in double-strength coffee. Use 2 teaspoons instant coffee to 2½ fluid ounces water.

Cherry Nut Chocolate Cake: Use Basic Recipe. Add 2-3 oz. quartered glacé cherries and

1 oz. chopped walnuts to the chocolate mixture. Fill with vanilla butter cream.

Exciting new fillings

Lemon banana cream: Use basic butter cream recipe but substitute 1½ tablespoons mashed banana and ½ tablespoon lemon juice for milk and vanilla. This is especially delicious when used to fill Mocha Cake.

Treacle Festival Cake

Mocha cream: Use basic butter cream recipe. Sift 1½ tablespoons cocoa with icing sugar. Use strong coffee instead of top of the milk. Use to fill cherry nut cake.

Lemon or orange cream: Use basic butter cream recipe but substitute lemon or orange juice for milk and grated rind of ½ lemon or 1 orange for vanilla. Use to fill Mocha Cake.

Orange Chocolate Cream: Melt 1½ oz. plain chocolate and beat into basic recipe after butter and sugar have been creamed. Substitute 1 heaped teaspoon grated orange rind for vanilla essence. Use for any of the variations on the basic cake recipe.

Extra special toppings

Glossy chocolate topping: Melt 5 oz. plain chocolate in a basin over a pan of hot water. Stir in ⅛ pint boiling cream. Cool and pour over cake.

Cream Cheese Topping: Soften 3 oz. cream cheese with a tablespoon of milk. Add 6 oz. icing sugar and 1 further tablespoon milk. Stir in 1 teaspoon vanilla essence and mix until blended. A delicious topping for the Chocolate Apple Cake.

Caramel Topping: Use a small, strong pan. Stir 4 oz. sugar in ¼ pint water over a low heat until sugar dissolves. Stop stirring and raise heat. Remove spoon and allow caramel mixture to boil rapidly. Continue to boil until mixture reaches a caramel colour.

TREACLE FESTIVAL CAKE

You require: 4 oz. butter • 3 oz. Barbados sugar • 1 tbsp. black treacle • 2 eggs • 6 oz. self-raising flour • ½ teasp. mixed spice • 3 tbps. milk • 2 oz. sultanas • For topping: 8 oz. icing sugar • about 2 tbsp. lemon juice • 2 oz. sugar • 1 tbsp. water • 1-2 oz. mixed shelled nuts, i.e., walnuts, cashew nuts, blanched almonds and unskinned hazel nuts •

Cream butter, sugar and treacle together until light and fluffy. Blend eggs and add to the mixture slowly so that it remains stiff. Fold in sieved flour and mixed spice, milk and sultanas. Turn into a 7 in. round greased and lined cake tin. Bake for about 1 hour at Mark 3, 335 deg. Remove from the oven and allow to cool slightly before turning out on to a wire tray.

To make topping, blend icing sugar with lemon juice to give a pouring consistency and pour over cake, allowing some of the icing to trickle down the sides. When set, lift on to a serving dish. Dissolve sugar in water in a pan, bring to the boil and boil rapidly for 1-2 minutes or until a pale caramel colour. Spoon the mixture quickly over the nuts and leave a few minutes to harden. Arrange nuts on top of cake. The photograph above left shows an attractive decorative pattern.

COOKED ICINGS AND OTHER DECORATIONS

Certain icings, although not difficult to make, entail heating or cooking the ingredients. Of these, the most generally used is American frosting. It has one great advantage, it never completely hardens under the crisp surface. It is not suitable for piping, however.

FROST 'N SNOW CAKE
Colour plate seven

You require: 1¼ lb. mixed glacé and crystallized fruits (cherries, pineapple, ginger, angelica, apricots, etc.) • 2 oz. almonds • 2 oz. walnuts • 8 oz. butter • 7 oz. sugar • 4 eggs • few drops almond essence • 10 oz. plain flour • ⅛ teasp. baking powder • pinch salt • For frosting: 1 lb. granulated sugar • ¼ pint water • pinch cream of tartar • 2 egg whites •

Grease and line an 8 in. round or 7 in. square cake tin. Cut all the glacé and crystallized fruits into pieces about the size of a third of a cherry. Mix with 1-2 tablespoons weighed flour. Blanch and chop almonds. Chop walnuts. Cream butter and sugar. Beat in eggs and a few drops of almond essence. Sift flour, baking powder and salt and fold into mixture. Finally fold in the prepared fruit and nuts. Put mixture into tin. Hollow out centre well, using the back of a wooden spoon. Bake at Mark 3, 335 deg., for 2¼-2½ hours.
To make frosting: Put sugar and water into a pan. Heat gently until sugar has dissolved. Add good pinch cream of tartar to the mixture in the pan. Bring to boil. Boil to temperature of 240 deg. or until a drop of syrup, dropped in cold water, forms a ball which is only just firm.

Whisk egg whites until stiff. Pour on hot syrup, a little at a time, whisking after each addition. Continue whisking until mixture holds soft 'peaks' – these should hold their shape when lifted. If too soft, the icing will slide off the cake. Spread over cake immediately, lifting peaks with tip of knife. Add decorations. Leave to set.

ROSE CAKE
Colour plate ten

You require: For cake: 4 oz. margarine • 4 oz. castor sugar • 2 eggs • 4 oz. self-raising flour, sieved • 3-4 drops vanilla essence • cochineal • For filling: 2 oz. butter • 4 oz. icing sugar • For frosting: 12 oz. granulated sugar • water • 2 egg whites • pinch cream of tartar • ½ teasp. vanilla essence • cochineal •

Cream margarine and sugar, beat in eggs and the essence. Lightly fold in flour, divide in half, colouring one portion pink. Turn into 2 greased and floured 7 in. sandwich tins. Bake at Mark 5, 375 deg., on the middle shelf for 20-25 minutes. For the filling, cream butter until white, beat in the sieved sugar a little at a time, adding a few drops of vanilla essence and cochineal, or 1 oz. melted chocolate or coffee essence to taste. Sandwich cakes together and cover with frosting, made in this way.
Put sugar and 3 tablespoons water into a bowl over boiling water. Add cream of tartar, egg whites and essence. Whisk hard for 7 minutes. Remove from heat, add colouring, beat until it is smooth and thick enough to spread over the cake.

SLIMMING CAKE
Colour plate nine

You require: For cake: 3 egg whites • 1 oz. castor sugar • 3 egg yolks • ¼ teasp. vanilla essence • 4 oz. self-raising flour, sifted twice • ½ teasp. liquid non-calorific sweetener to 3 tbsp. hot water • For filling: 8 oz. cottage cheese • ¼ teasp. liquid sweetener • lemon juice • cochineal • For frosting: 1 egg white • 1 teasp. gelatine • 4 oz. icing sugar • cochineal •

Whisk egg whites until stiff but not dry. Whisk in sugar, then egg yolks and essence. When thick and creamy fold in the sifted flour. Lastly, fold in liquid sweetener and turn into two 7-8 in. greased sandwich tins. Bake in moderately hot oven, Mark 5, 375 deg., for about 20 minutes. Turn on to a wire tray and allow to cool. When cold sandwich together with cream filling and decorate with frosting. To make a larger cake, double mixture and bake in three 7-8 in. tins, tinting one third of the mixture pink.

Make filling: rub cottage cheese through a sieve. Sweeten with liquid non-calorific sweetener, add lemon juice to taste. Tint pink. Sliced strawberries or shredded pineapple may then be added to taste, if desired.

Make frosting: Beat white of one egg until stiff. Add gelatine which has been dissolved in 5 tablespoons of hot water and allowed to cool, beating all the time. Beat in the icing sugar and tint pink. Spread over cake.

COFFEE FUDGE CHOCOLATE CAKE
Colour plate six

You require: 6 oz. butter • 6 oz. castor sugar • 4 medium eggs, separated • 1½ dessp. marmalade • 6 oz. plain chocolate • 6 oz. plain flour • ¾ level teasp. baking powder • 1½ oz. ground almonds • For coffee glacé fudge icing: 3 oz. butter • 12 oz. icing sugar • 2 tbsp. strong black coffee • For decoration: pistachio nuts •

Beat butter and sugar until creamy. Beat in egg yolks gradually, add marmalade. Stir in chocolate, already melted in basin over hot water. Fold in flour, baking powder, almonds, then stiffly beaten egg whites. Bake in a 7 in. greased cake tin at Mark 2, 310 deg., for 1¼-1½ hours. Cool, turn out.

Melt the butter with the coffee over moderate heat and, when just boiling, remove and beat in sugar. Cool a little and beat again. Pour over top of cake, spreading down sides with a warmed palette knife. Decorate with chopped pistachio nuts as illustrated in the colour plate.

Coffee Fudge Chocolate Cake

Frost 'n Snow Cake: Heat 1 lb. granulated sugar and ¼ pint water gently until sugar has dissolved. Add good pinch cream of tartar to mixture, bring to boil, boil to 240 deg. Whisk 2 egg whites till stiff, pour on hot syrup, a little at a time, whisking after each addition. Continue until mixture holds soft peaks. Spread on cake immediately. Lift peaks with tip of knife. Decorate as shown.

Mimosa Cake

CHOCOLATE FUDGE ICING

You require: 8 oz. granulated sugar • 3 tbsp. water •
1 oz. butter • 1 small can condensed milk • ½ oz.
cocoa •

Stir the sugar, water and butter in a pan over
gentle heat until the sugar has dissolved. Add the
milk, and allow mixture to boil steadily until a
small drop put into cold water forms a soft ball
(238 deg.). Add the cocoa and beat until mixture
is thick enough to spread. Immediately spread
over cake, making sure that you get it completely
coated while the icing is pliable enough. The cake
shown here is decorated with walnut halves,
pressed into place just before the icing sets.
This type of icing can easily be over-cooked and,
although it has a deliciously creamy texture if just
right, it loses this when cooked even a few minutes too long, so test frequently for the soft ball
stage, have the cake ready to be iced on a wire
tray, and work quickly once the icing is ready.

Other flavourings for Fudge Icing

Strong coffee can be used instead of water for
mocha icing, and the cocoa omitted for coffee
icing. Vanilla, almond or rum essences can be
added to the basic ingredients.

Step-by-step stages of making chocolate fudge icing

ICED GINGERBREAD SQUARES

You require: For gingerbread: 11 oz. self-raising flour • ½ teasp. salt • 1 teasp. ground ginger • 3 oz. soft brown sugar • 11 oz. black treacle • 4 oz. butter or margarine • ¼ pint milk • For butterscotch icing: 12 oz. demerara sugar • ¼ pint milk • 1 oz. butter or margarine • 1 teasp. vanilla essence • pinch bicarbonate of soda •

Grease a tin measuring 11½ in. × 8½ in. across the top and 8½ in. × 6 in. across the base and line the base with greaseproof paper. Sieve the dry ingredients into a mixing bowl. Melt the fat with the milk in a small saucepan, add the treacle.

Add the milk, etc., to the dry ingredients and stir thoroughly. Put the mixture into the prepared tin and bake at Mark 3, 335 deg., for 45-50 minutes. Make icing: Put the milk and sugar into a saucepan over a low heat. When the sugar is dissolved, boil briskly until a temperature of 230 deg. is reached. Remove the pan from the heat, add the butter, essence and bicarbonate of soda. Beat until the mixture thickens. Spread the icing over the cooked gingerbread and allow to set. Cut into squares. The squares may be decorated with chopped crystallized or stem ginger.

GINGERBREAD

You require: 4 oz. margarine • 6 oz. black treacle • 2 oz. golden syrup • ¼ pint milk • 2 eggs • 8 oz. plain flour • 2 oz. sugar • 1 rounded teasp. mixed spice • 1 level teasp. bicarbonate of soda • 2 level teasp. ground ginger •

Using a large saucepan, warm together margarine, treacle and syrup. Add milk and allow mixture to cool. Beat eggs and add to cooled mixture. Sieve dry ingredients together in a bowl, add the cooled mixture and blend in with a tablespoon. Turn into a greased and lined 7 in. square cake tin. Bake

Gingerbread

Iced Gingerbread Squares

on the middle shelf at Mark 2, 310 deg., for 1 ¼-1 ½ hours.

APPLE GINGERBREAD SURPRISE

You require: For topping: 2 oz. butter • 2 oz. brown sugar • 2 tart dessert apples, pared, cored and sliced • For cake: 4 oz. self-raising flour • ½ teasp. salt • 1½ level teasp. ginger • 1 level teasp. grated nutmeg • 4 oz. butter • 4 oz. soft brown sugar • grated rind of 1 lemon • juice of 1 lemon • 2 eggs •

Make topping: Cream together the butter and sugar spread over bottom and sides of an 8 in. cake tin, arranging apple slices evenly over the base. Make cake: Sift flour, salt and spices together; cream butter and sugar with the lemon rind and juice until light and fluffy. Beat in the eggs one at a time, fold in the sieved flour and spices and spread the mixture carefully over the apples. Bake at Mark 4, 350 deg., for 45 minutes. Turn on to a dish and decorate with cherries, if desired. Serve hot or cold with cream.

ORANGE UPSIDE-DOWN CAKE

You require: For decoration: 2 oranges • 4-5 glacé cherries • angelica • 7-8 blanched almonds, split • 1 oz. butter or margarine • 4 tbsp. golden syrup, warmed • For cake: 6 oz. super sifted self-raising flour • pinch salt • 1 oz. semolina • 1 level teasp. grated orange rind • 2½ oz. butter or margarine • 4 oz. castor sugar • 1 egg • 4 tbsp. milk • 2 tbsp. water •

Peel oranges, slice into rounds. Arrange on base of a greased 8 in. cake tin, put half a cherry in centres, fill up spaces with pieces of orange, almonds and angelica leaves. Boil fat and syrup for 3 minutes until light brown. Pour over fruit. Sieve flour and salt. Beat fat until soft, add sugar, beat again until light in colour and fluffy in texture. Add rind and egg with a tablespoon of flour, beat well. Beat in liquid in two stages, adding a little flour with each. Stir in rest of flour and semolina. Put into tin, smooth level. Bake at Mark 4, 350 deg., for 50 minutes.

MIMOSA CAKE
Colour plate eight

You require: 4 oz. butter or margarine • 4 oz. castor sugar • 2 eggs • 4 oz. self-raising flour • pinch salt • 1 tbsp. warm water • 1 teasp. grated orange rind • For filling: strawberry jam • For icing: 8 oz. granulated

Apple Gingerbread Surprise

sugar • 1 dessp. golden syrup • good pinch cream of tartar • 6 tbsp. cold water • 2 egg whites • 2 oz. icing sugar • 1 teasp. grated orange rind • ½ tbsp. orange juice • To decorate: Mimosa balls and pieces of angelica •

Make and bake as for Victoria Sandwich using orange rind to flavour cake. Sandwich layers together with strawberry jam. To make icing: put sugar, syrup, cream of tartar and water in pan. Heat gently to dissolve. Cover, simmer for 3 minutes. Remove lid and boil to 240 deg. or until a drop of syrup placed in cold water forms a ball that is only just firm. Whisk egg whites and then beat in sugar syrup little at a time, whisking well after each addition. Add rest of ingredients. Whisk until thick. Use to coat cake. Decorate with mimosa balls and angelica as shown in the colour plate.

CARAMEL ORANGE CAKE

You require: For orange sandwich: 6 oz. self-raising flour • 6 oz. butter • 6 oz. castor sugar • grated rind of 1 small orange • 3 eggs • For filling and topping: 4 oz. butter • 5 oz. soft brown sugar • juice 1 small orange • 10 oz. sieved icing sugar • a few orange jelly slices •

Well grease and line two 8 in. sandwich tins, sift flour. Cream butter and sugar and finely grated orange rind until light and creamy. Beat in blended egg gradually, keeping the mixture stiff. Add 1 tablespoon of the sifted flour to prevent curdling. Fold in remainder of the sifted flour and turn into prepared tins. Bake in the centre of the oven at Mark 5, 375 deg., for about 20-30 minutes. Cool on a wire rack.

Make filling and topping: Melt butter in a small saucepan over a low heat, add sugar and stir until dissolved, boil for 1 minute. Add juice and bring up to the boil. Remove from the heat at once. Cool until luke warm, beating in icing sugar. When all the icing sugar has been included, the mixture should form soft peaks when lifted up from the bowl. If it is a little too soft, chill for 10-15 minutes.

Sandwich the cakes together with one third of the mixture and spread the remainder over the top and sides. Fork a pattern over the whole surface and then decorate with orange slices.

CHOCOLATE FROSTED CAKE
Colour plate nine

You require: 3 oz. plain chocolate • 1 tbsp. milk • 6 oz. margarine • 6 oz. castor sugar • 4 eggs • 8 oz. flour (with plain flour add 2 level teasp. baking powder)

• chocolate butter icing • chocolate frosting • chopped blanched almonds •

Grease three 7 in. sandwich tins and dust with flour. Melt the chocolate in the milk. Cream the margarine and sugar until light and fluffy. Beat in the melted chocolate, then the eggs, one at a time. Sieve the flour and baking powder, if used, and lightly fold into the mixture. Divide the mixture into the prepared tins. Bake for approx. 20 minutes at Mark 5, 375 deg. Turn out on to a wire tray and leave until cold. Sandwich together with chocolate butter icing and cover with chocolate frosting, made as for Marble Cake. Decorate with chopped blanched almonds.

CARAMEL FROSTED SPONGE

You require: For sponge: 3 large eggs • 3 oz. castor sugar • 3 oz. self-raising flour • For filling and topping: 2 egg whites • 12 oz. dark soft brown sugar • 4 tbsp. water • good pinch cream of tartar •

Grease and line two 7 in. round sandwich tins. Take eggs at room temperature and whisk with sugar until mixture is light and creamy and the whisk leaves a trail when lifted out of mixture. Fold in sieved flour, using a metal spoon. Turn into pre-

Caramel Frosted Sponge

pared tins and level mixture by tipping tins from side to side. Bake in a hot oven, Mark 6, 400 deg., for about 12-15 minutes, until the sponge is beginning to shrink from the edges. Turn out on to a wire rack to cool. Split each sponge in two and sandwich them in layers with a third of the frosting and quickly swirl the remainder over the sponge top and sides.

To give the effect shown in the photograph, swirl round with the tip of the blade of a knife held upright on top of the cake, and run the blade down the side in parallel diagonal lines. Make frosting: Put egg whites, sugar, water and cream of tartar in a basin over a saucepan of simmering water. Stir until all the sugar has dissolved. With a rotary whisk, whip mixture until it stands up in peaks (about 7 minutes). Remove from heat and continue beating until a stiff consistency for spreading.

MARBLE CAKE

You require: 2 oz. plain chocolate • 12 oz. self-raising flour • ½ teasp. salt • 10 oz. butter • 5 eggs • For filling: 3 oz. butter • 3 oz. honey • 3 oz. finely chopped hazel nuts • For frosting: 1 lb. granulated sugar • ½ pint water • good pinch cream of tartar • 2 egg whites • 8 oz. plain chocolate, melted (for a pale chocolate frosting, use only 4 oz.) • For decoration: crystallized violets •

Line a 9 in. cake tin with greaseproof. Break chocolate and melt in basin over pan of hot water. Sift flour and salt together. Cream butter and sugar together. Beat in eggs, one at a time. Fold in flour, a third at a time. Spoon into prepared tin. Pour melted chocolate, in thin trickle, over top. Using spoon, lightly mix chocolate into cake mixture. Bake at Mark 4, 350 deg., for 1½-2 hours. Make filling: cream butter until soft. Add honey and nuts. Mix well. When cake is cold, cut in half and sandwich together with filling.

Make frosting: put sugar and water in pan. Heat until sugar dissolves. Add cream of tartar. Boil to 240 deg. or until a spot of syrup dropped in cold water forms a ball which is only just firm. Whisk egg whites until stiff. Pour on hot syrup, whisk well after each addition, until mixture holds soft peaks. Whisk in chocolate. Spread over cake. Decorate with crystallized violets.

GINGER GATEAU

You require: For cake: 10 oz. self-raising flour • 2 teasp. baking powder • ½ teasp. salt • 2 oz. cocoa • 8 oz. castor sugar or soft brown sugar • 4 eggs • ⅙ pint (approx. 10 tbsp.) vegetable oil • 5 tbsp. green ginger wine • For filling: ¼ pint double cream • ⅙ pint single cream • 1-2 pieces stem ginger, finely chopped • For frosting: 1 lb. granulated sugar • ½ pint water • good pinch cream of tartar • 2 egg whites • few drops cochineal • For decoration: chocolate vermicelli or grated chocolate •

Grease and line base of three 8 in. sandwich tins. Sift flour, baking powder, salt, cocoa and sugar into bowl. Add rest of cake ingredients. Mix gently with wooden spoon and then beat for 1-2 minutes. Put in tins. Bake at Mark 4, 350 deg., for 25-30 minutes.

Make filling: whisk double and single cream together until fairly thick. Fold in stem ginger. Use to sandwich cold cake layers together. Make frosting as for Marble Cake, omitting melted chocolate and adding few drops of cochineal instead. Spread over cake. Finally, sprinkle with chocolate vermicelli or grated chocolate.

More unusual frostings

Coffee Frosting. Put 2 tablespoons coffee essence, 2 oz. demerara sugar and 2 oz. castor sugar in a small pan. Heat gently until sugar dissolves, bring to boil, and boil briskly for 2½ minutes exactly. Meanwhile whisk 2 egg whites and a pinch of cream of tartar together until very stiff, then pour in hot syrup in a thin steady stream. Continue whisking until stiff enough to spread. (Enough to fill or cover an 8 in. sponge sandwich.)

Coffee Fudge Frosting. Cream 3 oz. butter with 6 oz. soft brown sugar. Beat in gradually 1 egg yolk and 1 tablespoon coffee essence.

Tested tips

1. For success, cooked icings must reach exactly the right temperature. The only way you can be sure not to overcook and spoil them is to test early and frequently.

2. The great advantage of cooked icings is that they stay softer longer than royal icing.

EASY PIPED DECORATIONS FOR GATEAUX

By using star, shell and writing tubes only, a great many easy but effective piped decorations can be achieved. No great skill is needed to make and decorate any of the cakes in this section.

UPSIDE-DOWN CAKE

You require: For topping: 1 oz. margarine • 16 apricot halves, drained • 2 oz. brown sugar • glacé cherries • whipped cream • For cake: 6 oz. self-raising flour • 4 oz. castor sugar • 1 teasp. finely grated lemon rind • 4 oz. butter or margarine • 2 eggs •

Melt the margarine and pour into a deep, well-greased sandwich tin, approximately 7 in. in diameter. Arrange the apricot halves, cut side down, attractively in the bottom of the tin, then sprinkle with sugar.
Make cake: Sift flour. Cream together fat and sugar till light and fluffy, then stir in the lemon rind. Add the eggs whole, beating thoroughly after each addition; and finally fold in the flour.

Put the mixture into the tin spreading evenly over the fruit. Bake for 15 minutes at Mark 5, 375 deg., and then for a further 45 minutes, or until the cake is well-risen and firm to touch, at Mark 3, 335 deg. Turn out, cool, then decorate by putting a glacé cherry in the middle of each apricot half and piping whipped cream with a small star tube round the edge of the cake and in the centre.

COFFEE PEARMAIN

You require: 7 in. sponge flan case • 1 medium can pears • 1 dessp. gelatine • ¾ pint strong black coffee • 1 egg white • 1 oz. icing sugar • ¾ pint double cream • few chopped walnuts •

Drain the pears well, reserve two well-shaped halves for the decoration. Line the sponge flan case with the rest of the pears, thinly sliced. Dissolve the gelatine in the coffee and cool. Whisk egg white until very stiff. Fold in the icing sugar. Whip the cream until it is moderately stiff.

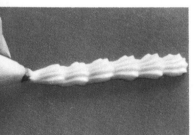

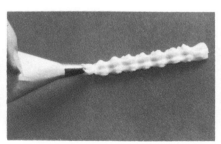
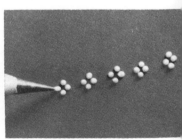

Upside-down Cake

Coffee Pearmain

Reserve a little for decoration. Add the beaten egg white to the remainder. When coffee is beginning to set, fold in the egg and cream mixture. Pour over the pears and leave to set. Using a large star tube, pipe rosettes of cream round the edge of the flan, and sprinkle with the chopped nuts. Before serving, decorate with more pear slices, cutting each pear half into three, and arranging

A no. 12 tube makes fine or thick shell edging and true lovers' knots; a no. 2 tube is used for dots, or trellis made by piping rows of lines parallel, then crossing hem at right angles

Windmill Gâteau

and bake at Mark 3, 335 deg., for 1 hour. Leave to cool in tin before turning out.

Split the cake and fill with some of the fresh cream. Spread a little cream around the edge and sprinkle with grated chocolate. To half the remaining cream, add the melted chocolate. Mark off the top into equal sections and pipe with alternate zigzags of plain and chocolate cream. Complete the decoration with cherries, pineapple and angelica, as shown in photograph bellow.

WINDMILL GATEAU
Colour plate eleven

You require: For cake: 8 oz. butter or margarine • 8 oz. castor sugar • 3 eggs • 10 oz. self-raising flour • 1 tbsp. coffee essence • 1 tbsp. cocoa • For butter cream: 8 oz. butter • 12 oz. icing sugar • 1 teasp. coffee essence • For decoration: cocoa • chocolate buttons • flaked almonds •

Grease and line the base of four 8 in. sponge tins. Cream the fat and sugar until light and fluffy. Beat in the lightly whisked eggs. Add the coffee. Carefully fold in the flour, adding enough warm water to form a soft dropping consistency. Now turn half the mixture into two of the prepared sponge tins.

To the rest of the mixture add the sieved cocoa and more water if necessary. Turn into the remaining tins. Bake at Mark 5, 375 deg., for 20 minutes.

them equally spaced like the spokes of a wheel round the cake.

The cake can be varied by using other varieties of canned fruit, such as peaches or pineapple.

AUSTRIAN GATEAU
Colour plate eleven

You require: For cake: 8 oz. plain chocolate • 3 tbsp. water • 8 oz. butter • 8 eggs, separated • 8 oz. ground almonds • 1 level tbsp. cornflour • 6 oz. castor sugar • For filling and decoration: Fresh cream • canned pineapple and cherries • 2 oz. plain chocolate, grated • 1 oz. plain chocolate, melted • angelica •

Slowly melt the 8 oz. chocolate with the water. Cream the butter until light and fluffy. Add the melted chocolate, beaten egg yolks, ground almonds and sugar. Continue to beat all the ingredients until light and creamy. Add the cornflour and beat again. Fold in the stiffly-beaten egg whites. Carefully put into a greased 9 in. cake tin

Austrian Gâteau

Almond Layer Cake

To make the butter cream, cream the ingredients together. Sandwich the layers together using one third of the coffee butter cream. Spread another third around the outer edge and dip into flaked almonds. Divide the remaining cream and add sufficient sieved cocoa to give a good chocolate flavour and colour. Use a sharp knife and mark the top off into twelve equal sections. Put the coffee and chocolate butter cream into two icing bags. Cut about ⅛ in. from the end of each. Start at the centre each time and pipe with a side to side movement using the colours alternately until the top is completely covered. Add halved buttons as shown.

ALMOND LAYER CAKE
Colour plate twelve

You require: For cake: 3 eggs • 3 oz. castor sugar • almond essence • 2½ oz. self-raising flour • ½ oz. cocoa • 1 tbsp. ground almonds • For filling: 4 oz. butter • 2 tbsp. ground almonds • almond essence • 2 tbsp. cold water • icing sugar • green food colouring • flaked almonds •

Whisk the eggs and sugar until thick and fluffy. Add few drops almond essence. Carefully fold in the sieved flour, cocoa and ground almonds. Pour into a greased and lined Swiss roll tin. Bake for about 15 minutes at Mark 5, 375 deg. Cool on a wire tray. Meanwhile prepare filling.

41

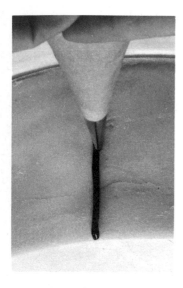

Pipe a line of icing from top to bottom with dark icing

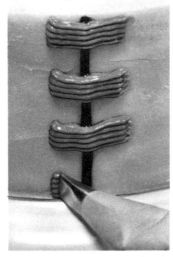

Cover the line with inch-wide bands of the paler icing

Pipe a second line close up to the bands using the dark icing

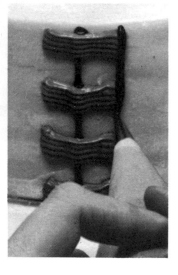

Pipe more bands over second line, filling in gaps left by first band

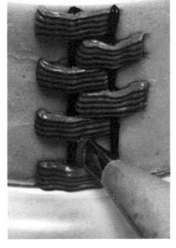

Make filling: Beat the butter and ground almonds together to a soft consistency. Add a few drops almond essence, cold water and sufficient sieved icing sugar to form a spreading consistency. Divide and colour one half pale green. Cut the cake into three equal pieces and sandwich together with plain almond cream. Spread cream evenly round the sides and dip into the flaked almonds. Using a star tube and a larger star for the green icing, decorate the cake as shown in the photograph.

FLORAL BASKET CAKE

You require: An 8 in. fruit cake, recipe on page 71 • 1½ lb. almond paste • cocoa • 2 egg whites • icing sugar • cochineal •

Coat the cake with almond paste reserving 2 oz. for marzipan flowers. Make icing: Mix 2 tablespoons cocoa to a smooth paste with a little boiling water and allow to cool. Beat egg whites with sufficient sugar to form a stiff icing. Add enough cocoa to obtain a pale chocolate colour. Take out 2 tablespoons of the mixture and add more blended cocoa to make a dark chocolate icing.

Ice, using a no. 3 writing tube. Pipe a line of dark icing from top to bottom of the cake. Now with the pale icing and a no. 9 fancy band tube, pipe inch-wide bands of icing over the original line. Return to the first icing and pipe another line alongside the other one, taking it close to the inch-wide bands. Complete the basket effect by piping bands over the second line of icing and in the spaces left by the previous bands. Continue like this right round the cake. Make a lid from cardboard and cover with the same basket-weave icing. Make a dozen roses out of the reserved almond paste which has been tinted pink. Arrange around edge of one side of the cake and prop lid on top.

BISCUIT GATEAU

You require: 2 eggs • 2 oz. icing sugar • 2 oz. butter • 8 oz. plain chocolate • 6 oz. broken sweet biscuits • 2 oz. chopped nuts • few drops brandy or vanilla essence • 4 oz. coffee butter cream •

Put the eggs and sugar into a basin and beat until thick and creamy. Gradually whisk in the melted butter and melted chocolate. Add the broken bis-

cuits – the pieces need to be small but larger than crumbs. Then add nuts and brandy or vanilla. Put into a tin, leave in a cold place until set. Turn out, decorate with rosettes of butter cream and chill again.

VIENNESE GATEAU

You require: For cake: 8 oz. self-raising flour • 6 oz. butter • 6 oz. castor sugar • ½ teasp. vanilla essence • 2 eggs • about 2 tbsp. milk • For mocha cream: 12 oz. icing sugar • 4 level tbsp. cocoa powder • 2 rounded teasp. instant coffee powder • 8 oz. butter or margarine • 3 tbsp. milk • For decoration: 6 pear halves, well drained • 1 oz. walnuts, chopped • a few walnut halves •

Sift flour twice. Beat the butter, sugar and essence to a smooth cream. Beat in eggs, one at a time. Stir in sifted flour and milk, mixing to a smooth, thick dropping consistency. Turn into 2 greased 8 in. sandwich tins. Bake at Mark 5, 375 deg., for about 30 minutes, until golden and springy to touch. Turn on to wire tray to cool. When cold split each cake in half.

Make mocha cream: Cream together all the ingredients until light and fluffy. Spread cream on the cake halves and sandwich layers together. Cover the top and sides of the cake with cream, then press the chopped walnuts against the sides. Arrange pear halves and walnuts on top and centre with a piped swirl of mocha cream. Chill in the refrigerator if possible before serving.

Tested tips

1. It is not advisable to pipe lettering in butter icing, but words can be spelt out by outlining the letters with small stars, close together.

43

Two-tier Lemon Gâteau

2. Butter icing is more suitable for piping bold designs with large tubes (no. 12, shell, or no. 13, five-star tubes) than delicate patterns.

3. The addition of liquid in the form of fruit juice or coffee can cause it to curdle. If you see this happening, do not add any more liquid but immediately beat in more icing sugar until smooth.

TWO-TIER LEMON GATEAU

You require: 1 lb. butter • 1 lb. castor sugar • 8 eggs • 6 teasp. grated lemon rind • 1 lb. 5 oz. plain flour • 2½ teasp. baking powder • ¼ teasp. salt • little milk • For icing: 12 oz. butter • 2 lb. icing sugar • 4 tbsp. lemon juice • silver balls •

Line one 7 and one 9 in. cake tin with grease-proof paper. Brush with oil or melted fat. Cream the butter and sugar together. Add the well beaten eggs a little at a time, beat well after each addition. Stir in lemon rind. Fold in the sifted flour, baking powder and salt. Add sufficient milk to give a soft, dropping consistency. Place mixture in the tins putting just under one-third into the 7 in. tin. Make a slight hollow in the centre of each cake; this will prevent unnecessary waste when

cakes are trimmed just before icing. Bake in centre of oven, at Mark 3, 335 deg. The 7 in. cake will take 1 hour 10 minutes to bake, the 9 in. cake 2 hours. When cooked, turn out on to cooling tray. Make butter icing by creaming butter with icing sugar, adding sufficient lemon juice to give a soft, smooth mixture. When cakes are quite cold cut level. Spread both with icing, reserve about one third to decorate, and place one on top of the other. Smooth the tops and sides of cakes. Using the rest of the icing, pipe garlands with a large shell tube as shown, shell-edge bases of both cakes and top with silver balls.

PINEAPPLE ICE CAKE

You require: 1 1lb. 14 oz. can pineapple rings • a few glacé cherries • boudoir biscuits • 1 pkt. pineapple instant whip • 1 pkt. dream topping • 1 pint milk •

Arrange slices of pineapple in the bottom of a 7 in. cake tin with a glacé cherry in the centre of each ring. Place boudoir biscuits around the sides of the tin. Reserve a tablespoon of dream topping powder for decoration, then combine the rest with the instant whip. Make according to the instant whip directions. Pour over the pineapple and place in the freezing section of the refrigerator for 3 hours. Turn out and decorate with dream topping, pineapple rings and glacé cherries.

Pineapple Ice Cake

PARISIAN GATEAU
Colour plate twenty-eight/nine

You require: For gâteau: 5 eggs • 5 oz. castor sugar •
5 oz. plain flour • 1½ tbsp. cocoa • pinch of salt •
For filling and decoration: 8 oz. butter • 1 lb. icing
sugar • warm water to mix • glacé cherries, halved •
angelica, cut in diamond shapes • 8 threepenny bars
milk chocolate • 1 sixpenny bar plain chocolate •

Whisk the eggs and sugar until thick, light and
fluffy. Carefully fold in the sieved flour, cocoa
and salt. Turn into three prepared 8 in. sandwich
tins, and bake at Mark 6, 400 deg., for 10-15 minutes. Cool. Meanwhile prepare the butter cream
by beating together the butter and icing sugar,
and adding a little warm water to form a smooth
consistency. Grate the plain chocolate on a coarse
grater. Cut the milk chocolate bars diagonally
with a sharp warm knife. Sandwich the sponge
layers together with a little butter cream and
spread an even coating round the sides. Roll the
sides in the grated chocolate. Spread more butter
cream evenly over the top and sprinkle on the
remaining grated chocolate. Mark off the top in
eight even sections, using a long knife. Continue
the markings down the sides of the gateau. Using a
large star tube fitted into a paper icing bag pipe
stars of butter cream in lines on each side of
the marks as illustrated. Press the halved chocolate
bars in between the lines of piped stars. Pipe a
rosette of cream at each join, and top with a
glacé cherry and diamonds of angelica. Finish with
a central rosette.

If you prefer not to use small chocolate bars as
part of the decoration, fill in the space between
parallel lines of butter cream rosettes with a piped
line of chocolate flavoured butter cream. Or, as
another alternative, use 16 narrow strips of angelica cut in 3 in. lengths.

*The elaborate design of the finished Parisian
Gâteau is really very simple to achieve as these
step-by-step photographs show. First spread butter
cream round side of the cake and roll it in grated
chocolate. Then cover top with butter cream and
sprinkle on remaining chocolate. Pipe stars of
butter cream and decorate with chocolate bars,
glacé cherries and angelica diamonds*

CONTINENTAL ORANGE GATEAU

You require: 4 oz. butter or margarine • 4 oz. castor sugar • 2 eggs • 4 oz. self-raising flour • pinch salt • 1 tbsp. warm water • 1 teasp. grated orange rind • For filling: 4 oz. butter • 8 oz. icing sugar • 1 tbsp. strained orange juice • For icing: 8 oz. icing sugar • 2 tbsp. strained orange juice • few drops orange food colouring • For decoration: 2 oz. tiny meringues • 4 oz. chopped toasted almonds • few orange pastilles • 1 oz. plain chocolate •

Make and bake cake as for Victoria Sandwich, adding orange rind to flavour basic mixture. Sandwich layers together with orange butter cream. Spread sides with rest of butter cream, roll in chopped almonds. Cover top with orange glacé icing. Using tiny dabs of icing, position miniature meringues round base and top edge of cake. Space the orange pastille sweets evenly round the top of cake, with a group in the centre.

Melt chocolate in a basin over hot water, taking care not to overheat it. Run a thin layer of melted chocolate on to a piece of waxed paper and allow to dry, and pour the rest of the chocolate in a zig-zag pattern over the meringues. Using a small fancy cutter, cut out nine chocolate shapes, ease off the waxed paper, and arrange as shown on cake.

GATEAU ROXALANNE

You require: For cake: 5 oz. self-raising flour • 1 oz. cornflour • 4 oz. castor sugar • 1 teasp. baking powder • ½ teasp. salt • 2 fl. oz. corn oil • ¼ pint cold water • 1 teasp. grated lemon rind • 1 teasp. lemon juice • 2 eggs yolks • 4 egg whites • ¼ teasp. cream of tartar • For icing and decoration: 8 oz. chocolate • 12 oz. icing sugar • 6 oz. butter • 2 egg yolks. • flaked almonds •

Grease a 7 in. tube cake tin. Sieve all the dry ingredients into a mixing bowl. Whisk together the corn oil, water, lemon rind, lemon juice and

Continental Orange Gâteau

egg yolks. Add to the dry ingredients and beat to form a smooth slack batter. Whisk the egg whites and cream of tartar until stiff and dry. Fold into the batter mixture. Turn into the prepared tin and bake at Mark 4, 350 deg., for 1 hour. When cooked, turn the tin upside down on a wire tray and leave until the cake cools. It will then slip out of the tin by itself.

Make the icing: Melt the chocolate in a basin over hot water. Cream the butter and sugar together until light and creamy. Beat in the egg yolks and melted chocolate. When the cake is cold, spread the sides with the chocolate icing. Roll edge of cake in flaked almonds. Spread more icing on top and pipe as shown with rosettes and lines.

STRAWBERRY CREAM GATEAU
Colour plate ten

You require: 6 oz. flour • ½ teasp. salt • 4 oz. butter • 4 oz. castor sugar • 2 eggs • 1 teasp. baking powder • ½ teasp. vanilla essence • milk • ⅟ pint stiffly whipped cream • ½ lb. fresh strawberries •

Sieve the flour, baking powder and salt together. Cream the butter and sugar thoroughly. Add the eggs gradually, beating well after each addition. Fold in the sieved flour using a metal spoon. Add a few drops of vanilla essence. Add sufficient milk to give a soft dropping consistency. Divide the mixture equally between two greased and floured sandwich tins and bake at Mark 4, 350 deg., for 25-30 minutes. When the cakes are cool, turn out and sandwich together with a little whipped cream and a few sliced strawberries. Fill in the edge of the gâteau between the two layers with halved strawberries and rosettes of whipped cream. Mark the outer rim of the top of gâteau in three equal segments, and arrange three strawberry whirls from the centre to these three points. Fill in space between whirls with piped rosettes of cream.

Gâteau Roxalanne

4 eggs • 1 tbsp. instant coffee and 1 tbsp. hot water, or 1 tbsp. coffee essence • For butter icing: 8 oz. butter • 1 lb. sieved icing sugar • vanilla essence • 1 teasp. each cocoa and instant coffee • 1 tbsp. warm water • For decoration: desiccated coconut •

Grease and line the base of three 8–9 in. sandwich tins. Sift flour, salt and cocoa together. Cream butter and sugar together until light and fluffy. Beat in eggs one at a time. Fold in flour a third at a time. Dissolve coffee in water, stir into cake mixture. Divide mixture between tins and bake at Mark 5, 375 deg., for about 30 minutes. Turn on to a wire tray to cool, remove paper.

To make icing, cream butter until soft. Mix in sieved icing sugar and beat well, add a few drops vanilla essence. Reserve 3 tablespoons icing for the top, and use rest to sandwich cake layers together and cover sides. Coat sides with coconut.

Divide icing for the top into two; leave one half white. To the other half add cocoa, and coffee dissolved in warm water. Stir until well mixed adding extra sieved icing sugar to give a similar consistency to the plain icing. Put a star pipe into an icing bag, carefully put the two coloured icings into the bag, making sure you have one colour on each side of the bag. Pipe rosettes of icing over top of cake to give a two-tone effect.

SWISS MOUNTAIN LOG

You require: For Swiss roll: 4 oz. plain flour • 1 level teasp. baking powder • 3 medium eggs • 3 oz. castor sugar • 1 tbsp. hot water • 2 tbsp. red jam, warm • 12 oz. chocolate and 2 oz. plain butter cream •

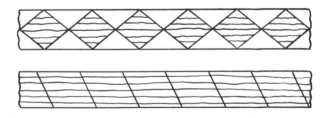

Easter Day Gâteau: Like many other cakes, this one is decorated with wings of angelica. Here are two ways to cut diamond shapes from a strip of angelica, first washed in warm water to soften

EASTER DAY GATEAU

You require: For cake: 6 oz. butter • 6 oz. castor sugar • rind and juice of an orange, grated • 3 eggs • 6 oz. self-raising flour • 1 oz. almonds • For filling and topping: ½ pint double cream • 1 oz. castor sugar • 4 oz. almond paste • 2 drops orange food colouring • 8 cloves • angelica • 2 oz. toasted almonds

Grease and line a 7 in. square cake tin. Cream together butter, sugar, orange rind and juice until light and fluffy. Blend eggs and add a little at a time, beating well after each addition. Skin and finely chop the almonds. Fold sifted flour and chopped nuts into creamed mixture. Turn into prepared tin and bake at Mark 5, 375 deg., for about 1¼ hours. Allow to cool completely and split in half.

Make filling and topping: Whip cream with sugar. Put one third of the cream between layers of cake. Spread the rest on top of cake and around the sides. Decorate top of cake with a circle of marzipan oranges.

Make marzipan oranges: Colour almond paste with orange food colouring. Divide into eight and mould into balls. Lightly mark with a knife to represent orange skin. Stick a clove into top of each ball and make leaves of angelica. Cover sides of cake with toasted almonds.

MOCHA GATEAU

You require: 8 oz. self-raising flour • ½ level teasp. salt • 1 tbsp. cocoa • 8 oz. butter • 8 oz. castor sugar •

Slimming Cake

Orange Butterfly

Chocolate Frosted Cake

Rose Cake

Strawberry Cream Gâteau

Swiss Mountain Log

Sift together flour and baking powder. Whisk eggs and sugar in a bowl over basin or pan of hot water till thick and creamy and until mixture holds its own weight. Fold in flour and baking powder lightly with a metal spoon and lastly stir in hot water, working as quickly as possible. Pour mixture into a greased, shallow tin, approx. 12 in. × 9 in., lined with greased paper. Bake towards top of oven at Mark 7, 425 deg., for 7-9 minutes. Turn out on to greaseproof paper sprinkled with castor sugar and, resting on top of a damp tea-towel, trim away crisp edges with a sharp knife then spread Swiss roll with jam. Roll up tightly and cool on a wire tray. Make chocolate butter cream. Cut a 1½ in. diagonal piece off one end of the Swiss roll, a third of the way along, securing with a little chocolate butter cream.

Cover ends of large and small logs with plain butter cream and, using a No. 3 writing tube and bag, decorate with rings of chocolate butter cream. Cover rest of log all over with chocolate butter cream and ridge with prongs of a fork for roughened effect. Shower with 'snow' using sieved icing sugar and decorate as liked with robins and sprigs of holly or any Christmasy ornaments of your choice. (On page 109 you will find a recipe for a plainer log cake.)

CHOCOLATE ALMOND CREAM SPONGE

You require: For cake: 3 eggs • 3 oz. castor sugar • 3 oz. self-raising flour • 1 dessp. cocoa • For butter cream: 8 oz. icing sugar • 6 oz. butter or margarine • almond essence • green colouring • cocoa • chopped pistachio nuts •

49

Chocolate Almond Cream Sponge

Whisk eggs and sugar together until thick and creamy. Sieve together cocoa and flour and lightly fold into eggs and sugar. Turn into two greased 7 in. sandwich tins and bake at Mark 5, 375 deg., for about 25 minutes. When cooked cool on a wire tray.

Make butter cream: Beat the icing sugar and butter or margarine together. When light and fluffy take out about two tablespoons and add sufficient sieved cocoa to give a chocolate flavour and colour. Mix the essence and colouring into the remainder. Sandwich the cakes together with a layer of butter cream. Spread some round the sides and roll in chopped nuts. Cover the top and pipe on chocolate butter cream as illustrated.

CHOCOLATE MUSHROOM CAKE

You require: For cake: 3 oz. castor sugar • 3 eggs • ½ teasp. almond essence • 2½ oz. self-raising flour • 1 level tbsp. cocoa • 2 oz. ground almonds • sieved jam • For almond paste: 6 oz. ground almonds • 6 oz. castor sugar • 1 small egg yolk • For butter cream: 3 oz. butter • 6 oz. icing sugar • 1 tbsp. sieved cocoa • almond essence •

Whisk the sugar, eggs and essence until light and fluffy. Fold in the sieved flour and cocoa. Carefully add the ground almonds. Turn into a greased 9 in. sandwich or cake tin. Bake for 25 minutes in oven at Mark 5, 375 deg. Cool on a wire tray. Brush the sides with sieved jam.

Roll almond paste into a strip, long and deep enough to cover the sides. Press into position and trim. Knead trimmings into a roll for the stalk. To make the butter cream, beat the icing sugar and butter together until smooth. Beat in the almond essence and sieved cocoa. Using a star tube, pipe lines from the outer edge to the centre as shown in the photograph and place the stalk in the centre.

If preferred, the top of this rather rich and unusual cake can be finished in other ways. The whole of the top can be covered with rosettes, piped close together with a large star tube. Or the top can be spread smoothly with a fairly thick layer of the butter cream, and the remainder stiffened by beating in a little extra sieved icing sugar for piping a more elaborate decoration. In this case it will not be necessary to reserve almond paste trimmings.

Chocolate Mushroom Cake

PASTRIES AND MERINGUES

A great variety of delicate and elaborate pastries for afternoon tea can be made with choux paste, and it is not really as difficult as many housewives think. There are two points during the preparation of choux pastry cases, when the inexperienced cook may think she has a failure on her hands, although in fact there is nothing wrong with the pastry. The first is when the egg yolks or eggs are added to the smooth soft paste which results from beating the flour well into the mixture of boiling water, salt and fat. The mixture does appear to curdle and seems as though it will never become smooth, but providing the first egg is added while the mixture is still hot enough to cook it slightly, a little patience and vigorous beating will put this right. The second danger point comes when the cook discovers that the pastry has puffed up well and is the right colour, but seems doughy inside. Undercooked choux

pastry cases tend to collapse, but any uncooked choux paste can be scraped out of the cases before they are filled, providing outside is crisp and set.

STRAWBERRY PUFFS
Colour plate fourteen

You require: 2 oz. butter • ¼ pint water • pinch salt • 3 oz. plain flour • 2 large eggs • For filling: cream • strawberries or fruit in season • chocolate icing •

Bring the fat, water and salt to the boil in a saucepan. Add the flour, remove the pan from the heat and beat until smooth. Cool slightly, beat in the eggs one at a time. Spoon dessertspoons of the mixture on to a greased baking sheet, bake at Mark 7, 425 deg., for approximately 30-40 minutes. Slit and cool. Fill with whipped cream and fruit, e.g. pineapple and cherries, strawberries, or any fruit in season. Coat with chocolate icing.

CHOCOLATE ECLAIRS

You require: For éclair cases: 2 oz. butter or margarine • ¼ pint cold water • pinch salt • 3 oz. plain flour • 2 large eggs • For filling: whipped cream • For chocolate icing: 1 dessp. cocoa • 4 tbsp. water • 6 oz. icing sugar • small knob butter • ½ tspn. vanilla essence •

Bring the water, fat and salt slowly to the boil, and immediately add all the flour. Beat until mixture leaves the side of the pan. Remove from heat and when cool, beat in the eggs one at a time. Using a ½ in. plain piping tube, pipe on to a greased baking tray in even lengths approx. 4-5 in. long. Bake in an oven Mark 7, 425 deg., for 25-30 minutes. Slit and cool. Fill with whipped cream. Coat with chocolate icing.

Make icing: Blend cocoa and water. Cook in saucepan until it thickens. Add the knob of butter and allow to cool. When cold, add the sieved icing sugar, and vanilla essence, to form a thick coating consistency.

COFFEE ECLAIRS

You require: 12 éclair cases, made as for chocolate éclairs • 8 oz. coffee flavoured glacé icing • For filling: ½ pint milk • ¾ oz. cornflour • 1 tbsp. castor sugar • 2 egg yolks • 1 teasp. coffee essence or instant coffee mixed with 1 tbspn. hot water •

Blend the cornflour with the milk, stir in the egg yolks and sugar, and cook over a gentle heat until thick. Beat in the coffee essence. Cool. Fill

into an icing bag with a plain tube, make a hole at the end of each éclair case and fill with the cream. Coat the tops of the éclairs with coffee flavoured glacé icing.

CREAM BUNS

You require: For buns: 2 oz. super sifted self-raising flour • pinch salt • 1 oz. butter or margarine • ⅛ pint water • 1-2 eggs • For filling: ½ pint double cream • 1 teasp. castor sugar • 2 drops vanilla essence • icing sugar •

Sieve flour and salt on to a piece of paper. Bring fat and water to the boil in a small pan. Remove from heat, add flour all at once. Stir quickly with a wooden spoon until mixture forms a ball of

Coffee Eclairs

Chocolate Eclair

dough. Add one egg, beat until absorbed. If necessary, add a little more beaten egg until mixture can be pulled up into soft points with the spoon. Beat again very thoroughly until smooth. Grease base of 2 round shallow cake or biscuit tins, about 10 in. in diameter with well fitting lids. Put 7 teaspoons mixture in each tin about 2 in. apart, leaving surface rough to make peaks in the buns. Put lids in position, place one tin on top of other and bake at Mark 7, 425 deg., unopened for 45 minutes, reversing position of tins half way through. If tins with lids are not available, use greased roasting tins closely covered with foil. Make filling: Beat ½ pint double cream, add castor sugar and vanilla essence. Cut buns in half and pile in the filling. Replace tops and dust with icing sugar. Alternatively, the buns can be filled with slices of ice cream or fresh fruit and whipped cream.

CHOCOLATE SWANS

You require: For swan shapes: 2 oz. butter or margarine • ¼ pint water • pinch salt • 4 oz. plain flour • 2 large eggs • For filling and decoration: whipped fresh cream • 2 oz. plain chocolate • 2 tbsp. milk and water • 4 oz. icing sugar.

Bring the fat, salt and water to the boil. Add the flour and beat until the mixture forms a ball leaving the pan clean. Remove from the heat and beat until smooth, and cool. Beat in the eggs separately. Put a ¼ in. plain tube in to an icing bag and add half the mixture. Pipe 'S' shapes to form swans' necks and heads on to a greased baking sheet. Place the remaining mixture on the baking tray in spoonfuls to make the bodies. Bake at Mark 6, 400 deg., for 20 minutes or until golden brown. Allow to cool on a wire tray. Make chocolate icing: Melt the chocolate with the milk and water in a basin over a pan of hot water. Add the icing sugar and beat until smooth. To decorate, make the wings by cutting off the top of the body. Cut in two and coat each half with the chocolate icing. Scoop out the inside of the body (which may contain a little uncooked choux paste) and fill with the cream. Place the neck of the swan in the cream. Replace wings and put two dots of chocolate icing for the eyes.

Chocolate Swans

CHOUX PASTRY FOR TEA FANCIES

You require: 2 oz. flour • good pinch salt • 8 tbsp. water • 4 tbsp. vegetable oil • 2 eggs •

Sift the flour and the salt on to a plate. In a pan bring the water to the boil and add the flour and oil together. Beat well over the heat until the mixture forms a stiff, smooth paste and leaves the sides of the pan clean. Remove from the heat. Let this mixture cool slightly before adding the eggs, one at a time, beating hard after each addition, until the mixture is smooth and glossy.

Eclairs: Place the choux pastry in an icing bag fitted with a ½ in. plain pipe. Pipe 3 in. lengths of the choux pastry on to an ungreased baking sheet. Bake at Mark 6, 400 deg., for 25-30 minutes. When cold, split the éclairs and fill with strawberries, sliced if large, sprinkled with a little sugar and with a layer of lightly whipped cream. Ice with melted plain or milk chocolate or with chocolate or coffee glacé icing. Makes 12-14.

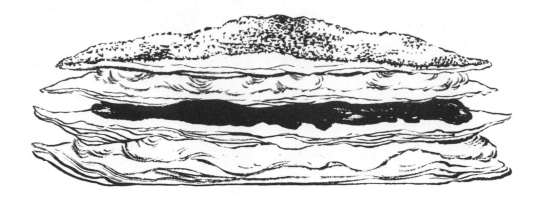

Pastry Puffs: Drop dessertspoonfuls of the pastry on to ungreased baking sheets, 2 inches apart. Bake in oven, Mark 6, 400 deg., for 35-45 mins. Cool. Split and fill with strawberries, sliced if large, sprinkled with sugar and with a layer of lightly whipped cream. Makes 10-12.

QUICK FLAKY PASTRY

You require: 1 lb. flour • ½ teasp. salt • 5 oz. vegetable fat • 5 oz. margarine • about ¼ pint cold water •

This is the pastry to use for topping pies, making pastries, turnovers, cream or fruit triangles and slices. Instructions are lettered to help you. **A.** Sift flour and Salt. **B.** Mix vegetable fat and margarine together. **C.** Rub in one quarter of fat and mix to a soft, not sticky, dough with the cold water. **D.** Knead lightly. **E.** Roll out to oblong, about 20 in. × 10 in. **F.** Spread rest of fat over two-thirds of dough. **G.** Fold plain third up over centre and top third down over centre. **H.** Seal edges. Leave, covered, in cool place for half an hour. **I.** Roll out again to large oblong, keeping folded edges to sides. Roll up loosely like a Swiss roll. Seal ends. Cover, leave for half an hour. Roll out and use as required.

Cream Triangles: Roll out 1 lb. flaky pastry, about ¼ in. thick, to an oblong 20 in. × 10 in. Trim edges. Cut into 3 in. squares. Cut each square in half to form two triangles. Place on baking sheets. Brush 12 triangles with water and sprinkle with castor sugar. Bake at Mark 7, 425 deg., for 10-15 mins. When cold, sandwich together three layers with whipped cream. Top with sugared layer. Makes 12.

PARTY MERINGUES

You require: 3 egg whites • 6 oz. castor sugar • pink food colouring • For filling: whipped cream •

Put the egg whites into a bowl and whisk until very stiff. Whisk half the sugar into the mixture, fold in the remaining sugar. Tint half the meringue mixture pink. Pipe or spoon on to a greased and floured baking tray. Dry out in a cool oven, taking care not to overheat and change colour, for about one hour. Remove from baking tray with palette knife, cool on wire tray and put pink and white halves together with cream.

MERINGUE GATEAU
Colour plate thirteen

You require: For cake: approximately 36 sponge fingers • 1½ gills strong coffee • 1 tbsp. sherry or Tia Maria • For filling: 3 oz. butter • 3 oz. sieved icing sugar • 1½ oz. cocoa • 2-3 oz. chopped hazel nuts • 1 egg yolk • small amount of coffee or milk • For decoration: ¼ pint thick cream • 1 egg white • 1 oz. icing sugar • few drops vanilla essence • approximately 12 meringues (see recipe above) • square of chocolate, grated • hazel nuts •

Line an 8 or 9 in. cake tin with a round of greaseproof paper. This cake is easier to remove if a tin with a loose base is used. Pour the coffee and sherry or Tia Maria into a shallow dish. Dip enough of the sponge fingers into this to cover

Chocolate Meringues

Meringue Gâteau

the bottom of the tin – you will need to cut some to fit. Do not make the sponge fingers too soft. Make the filling by creaming the butter and icing sugar, then beating in the sieved cocoa, the egg yolk and nuts. Add just enough coffee or milk

to make a soft consistency. Spread half of this over the sponge fingers. Cover with more sponge fingers, the rest of the filling, and then a final layer of sponge fingers. Leave for several hours, or this cake can be stored in a refrigerator for some days. Turn out and remove the paper.

Whip the egg white until very stiff and whip the cream. Fold the egg white into the cream, then add the sugar and vanilla essence. Coat top and sides of the cake with the cream mixture, and press meringues round the sides. Decorate with grated chocolate, hazel nuts, and if any cream remains, with whirls of this on top of the cake. Serve as cold as possible.

CHOCOLATE MERINGUES

You require: 2 egg whites • 4 oz. castor sugar • 2 teasps. cocoa • For filling: fresh cream or butter cream •

Put the egg whites into a bowl and whisk until very stiff. Sieve together the cocoa and half the sugar. Beat this into the mixture. Fold in the remaining sugar. Pipe or spoon on to a greased and floured baking tray. Put into cool oven, Mark ¼, 240 deg., and bake until dry throughout. When cool store meringues in a tin until required. Just before serving sandwich together with fresh cream or butter cream.

If preferred, the meringues can be sandwiched together with ice-cream and topped with cream.

CHOCOLATE HAZEL NUT LAYER

You require: 8 oz. castor sugar • 1 rounded dessp. cocoa • 4 egg whites • 2 oz. hazel nuts • ½ pint double cream • grated chocolate •

Mark circles 7 in. in diameter on to three pieces of greaseproof paper on three baking sheets. Oil thoroughly. Sieve the sugar and cocoa together. Whisk the egg whites until stiff and then whisk in half the sugar and cocoa. Gradually fold in the remaining half. Pipe the meringue on the marked circles with a ½ in. icing tube or spread it over. Cook in a slow oven, Mark ½, 265 deg., for approximately 2-3 hours or until the meringues are dry throughout. Carefully remove from paper and turn on to a wire tray to cool. Chop the hazel nuts, keeping back a few for decoration. Whip the cream until stiff. Sandwich meringue layers together with cream and chopped nuts. Spread cream on the top and decorate with whole nuts and grated chocolate.

Tested tips

1. Meringues are simple to prepare, yet they can go wrong in cooking. The mixture must be dry and firm, not over-heavy with sugar causing it to spread and loose shape in the oven. Increase the proportion of egg white to sugar to make firmer.

2. A pinch of cream of tartar added with the sugar makes a more solid meringue. Sprinkle the tops with castor sugar before cooking to give a crisp finish.

3. The tops of meringues may be cooked while they are still syrupy underneath. Loosen from the tin with a palette knife, turn over and dry off until the underneath becomes completely dry.

4. The most common cause of failure is over-colouring. Remember the oven cannot be too cool. Try to reduce heat to the absolute minimum and be patient if your meringues take anything up to three hours to dry out fully, provided they do not discolour.

5. To prevent sticking, line baking sheet with greaseproof paper and oil this. Alternatively oil or grease and flour the baking sheet itself.

Chocolate Hazel Nut Layer

Windmill Gâteau

Austrian Gâteau

Almond Layer Cake

Meringue Gâteau

Strawberry Puffs

Strawberry Meringue Gâteau

COCONUT MERINGUES

You require: 3 egg whites • 6 oz. castor sugar • 3 oz. desiccated coconut • little butter or oil •

Whisk the egg whites until very stiff then gradually beat in 2 oz. of the sugar. When mixture is stiff again, fold in rest of sugar and the coconut with a metal spoon. Brush 2 baking sheets with melted butter or oil, place spoonfuls of the mixture on the baking sheets and cook about 2 hours at Mark ½, 265 deg., or Mark ¼, 240 deg., until firm. To remove from the tin, dip a palette knife in hot water, shake dry then slip under the meringues. Allow to cool on wire trays before storing in an airtight tin. These are very good sandwiched with ice cream.

STRAWBERRY MERINGUE GATEAU

You require: 6 eggs • 6 oz. castor sugar • 6 oz. flour • pinch salt • 2 tbsp. warm water • For meringues: 2 egg whites • 4 oz. castor sugar • To decorate: strawberry jam • strawberries • ½ pint whipped cream •

Line and grease three 8 in. × 11 in. Swiss roll tins. Whisk eggs and sugar together until thick (the mixture should be thick enough to hold a 'trail' from the whisk for 3-5 seconds). Using a metal spoon carefully fold in the sifted flour and salt and finally the warm water. Divide the mixture equally between the three tins and bake for 10-15 minutes at Mark 7, 425 deg.

Turn out and allow to become quite cold. Cut out 5 rounds, 4, 5, 6, 7 and 8 in. across. Make the meringues by whisking the egg whites until very stiff. Add 1 oz. of the sugar and whisk again until the mixture stands up in peaks. Fold in the remaining sugar. Pipe tiny meringues on to lightly oiled greaseproof paper placed on a baking sheet. Bake for about an hour at Mark ½, 265 deg., until crisp but still white. Remove from the paper with a warmed palette knife and allow to cool.

Sandwich the layers of sponge together with strawberry jam and place on a serving dish. Cover the cake with whipped cream. Decorate with strawberries and tiny meringues. Top with several strawberries and serve extra whipped cream separately. Serves 12-15. Although this is ideal for parties, you can make a small gâteau on the same lines, by reducing the quantities.

57

STRAWBERRY MERINGUE BOATS

You require: For boats: 3 egg whites • 6 oz. castor sugar • 3 level teasp. cocoa • For decoration: fresh cream • strawberries •

Whisk the egg whites until very stiff. Whisk in the sieved cocoa and half the sugar. Fold in the remaining sugar. Using large icing bag and a star tube, pipe oval shapes on to a greased and floured tray. Bake at Mark ¼, 240 deg., until crisp and dry throughout. Store in an airtight tin until required. Decorate with whipped cream and strawberries before serving.

SUMMER SNOWBALLS

You require: 2 egg whites • 5 oz. castor sugar • 2 oz. ground almonds • 2 oz. desiccated coconut • 1 oz. cornflour • little water • icing sugar •

Beat egg whites until stiff, then add rest of ingredients together with enough water to make the mixture a little softer than an ordinary meringue.

Arrange rice paper on 2 ungreased baking sheets – or if you have no rice paper use oiled greaseproof. Put spoonfuls of the mixture on the baking sheets, rounding them with a spoon. Bake at Mark 3, 335 deg., for 30 minutes. When cooked and still hot, dredge liberally with icing sugar. Allow to cool, then cut round the rice paper with sharp scissors. You will find it easy to remove snowballs from greaseproof.

MOCHA MERINGUES

You require: 1 oz. milk chocolate • 1 teasp. instant coffee • 3 egg whites • 6 oz. castor sugar •

Line baking sheets with greaseproof paper and brush with oil. Break chocolate into pieces and melt in basin over pan of hot water. Stir in instant coffee. Whisk egg whites stiffly. Add half sugar and whisk again until stiff. Fold in rest of sugar and chocolate mixture. Drop spoonfuls of mixture on to baking sheets to dry out, at Mark ¼, 240 deg.

Meringue Boats

PETITS FOURS AND OTHER SMALL CAKES

BASIC INGREDIENTS FOR PETITS FOURS

Genoese Sponge

You require: 3 eggs • 6 oz. castor sugar • 1½ tbsp. water • 3½ fl. oz. corn oil • 5 oz. plain flour • 1 oz. cornflour • 1 teasp. baking powder •

Grease and line two 8 in. × 10½ in. Swiss roll tins. Beat eggs, sugar and water in a bowl over hot water until thick and creamy. Remove from the heat and stir in the corn oil. Sieve the flour, cornflour, and baking powder. Fold lightly into egg mixture. Turn into prepared tins, bake at Mark 5, 375 deg., for 25 minutes. Remove from the tins and leave to cool on wire trays.

Almond Paste

You require: 8 oz. ground almonds • 4 oz. castor sugar • 4 oz. icing sugar • few drops of almond essence • little lemon juice • 1 egg or 3 egg yolks •

Sieve together the ground almonds and the sugars. Add the almond essence and lemon juice to beaten egg. Stir into the dry ingredients. Knead lightly until smooth. To colour almond paste, knead the colouring into the paste gradually until the required colour is produced.

Fondant

You require: 2 oz. glucose syrup • 1 egg white • 1 lb. icing sugar • flavouring • colouring • For decoration: cherries • angelica •

Warm the glucose slightly. Beat egg white lightly and add to syrup. Gradually stir in sieved icing sugar until a stiff paste is formed. Knead to a smooth dough and flavour and colour as required. Roll out to ½ in. thickness. Cut into fancy shapes. Decorate and leave on a wire rack overnight.

Decorations: Glacé cherries, angelica, walnuts, hazel nuts, almonds, chocolate vermicelli, crys-

Petits Fours

tallized violets, almond paste shapes, glacé icing and so on.

Variations using the Basic ingredients

Iced Petits Fours: Cut small shapes from Genoese sponge – rings, squares, triangles etc. Brush the tops and sides with warm, sieved apricot jam, cover with a thin layer of almond paste. Coat with glacé icing and decorate. These can be varied with different coloured icings, and decorations to your requirements.

Spirals: Shape balls of almond paste. Coat with pale yellow icing. Allow to set. Using a plain writing tube, pipe spirals of coffee flavoured icing starting right at the top of the ball and working downwards.

Stuffed Dates: Slit whole dates along the top and remove stone. Fill with green almond paste and decorate with a blanched almond.

Trefoils: Make three long rolls of different coloured almond paste. Brush with sieved apricot jam and stick together, two side by side and one on top. Brush all over with apricot jam and coat with chocolate vermicelli. Cut into ½ in. slices.

Chocolate Rum Truffles

You require: 2 oz. Genoese crumbs, rubbed through a fine sieve • 2 oz. chocolate, grated • 1 tbsp. chocolate powder • little orange juice • ½ teasp. apricot jam • rum to flavour • chocolate vermicelli •

Mix together all the ingredients except the chocolate vermicelli. Use rum to flavour and enough orange juice to make a soft but pliable mixture. Form into small balls and roll in chocolate vermicelli. Leave to harden.

Piped Fours

You require: 6 oz. ground almonds • 1 oz. cornflour • 7 oz. icing sugar • 1 egg • vanilla essence •

Mix together almonds, cornflour and sugar. Whisk together the egg and vanilla essence. Add to the dry ingredients and mix to form a smooth stiff paste. Pipe in small shapes on to greased greaseproof paper. Decorate with small pieces of glacé cherry, angelica or nuts. Bake at Mark 7, 425 deg., for 6-8 minutes until golden brown. Remove from paper and cool.

Choux Puffs

You require: ⅟ pint corn oil (approximately 3½ tbsp.) • ¼ pint water • 2½ oz. plain flour • ½ oz. cornflour • 2 teasp. sugar • pinch salt • 2 eggs • jam • icing sugar •

Heat the corn oil and water to boiling point in a saucepan. Remove from heat and add the sieved flour, cornflour, sugar and salt. Blend well together. Beat until the mixture forms a ball which leaves the side of the pan. Leave to cool for a few minutes. Beat in the eggs one at a time. Pipe the mixture in small rounds on a lightly greased baking sheet. Bake at Mark 6, 400 deg., for 20 minutes. When cool pipe a little jam through a slit in the base. Sprinkle with icing sugar.

Frosted Grapes

You require: 6 oz. castor sugar • 2½ fl. oz. water • black and white grapes •

Dissolve the castor sugar in the water over a low heat. Stir till dissolved, then boil until syrup begins to caramelize. Dip the grapes into the syrup individually. Allow excess syrup to drain off then roll all or half of each grape in castor sugar. Leave on greased, greaseproof paper to set.

RICH CHOCOLATE TRUFFLES

You require: 2 oz. butter • 2 oz. castor sugar • almond essence • 3 oz. ground almonds • 2 teasp. sieved cocoa • 2 teasp. sieved jam • sieved cake crumbs • rum or sherry • sieved jam • chocolate vermicelli or chopped nuts •

Cream the fat and sugar until soft and fluffy. Add the almond essence, almonds, cocoa and jam.

Beat thoroughly. Mix in sufficient cake crumbs to form a stiff paste.

Add a few drops of rum or sherry to flavour. Knead well, and roll into a sausage shape. Cut into equal-sized pieces. Roll each into a smooth ball. Cover with a thin layer of jam. Roll in chocolate vermicelli or chopped nuts.

CHOCOLATE FUDGE

You require: ½ pint milk • 1 lb. castor sugar • 1 tbsp. cocoa • knob of butter •

Measure the milk into a saucepan and add the sugar. When the sugar has dissolved over a low heat, add the cocoa and butter. Bring to the boil and boil gently until 240 deg. is reached or until, when a little of the mixture is dropped into cold water, it turns into a soft ball. Remove from the heat and beat well. When in thickens turn into an oiled tin. Leave to set and cut into squares.

CHOCOLATE CREAM SHELLS
Colour plate sixteen

You require: For shells: 3 oz. butter • 3 oz. castor sugar • ½ egg • 4½ oz. flour • 1 dessp. cocoa • For filling: fresh cream • For topping: icing sugar •

Chocolate Truffles

Cream the butter and sugar until light and fluffy. Add the egg. Fold in the sieved flour and cocoa. Mix well. Place in a forcing bag fitted with a large star nozzle, and pipe shell shapes on to a greased baking tray. Bake in oven Mark 5, 375 deg., for 15 minutes. Cool on a wire tray. Sandwich together with cream. Sprinkle with icing sugar.

ORANGE BUTTERFLIES
Colour plate nine

You require: 5 oz. super sifted self-raising flour • ¼ teasp. salt • 4 oz. castor sugar • 3 oz. vegetable cooking fat • 2 eggs • 1 tbsp. milk • rind of 1 orange or lemon, grated • For filling: 4 oz. icing sugar • 1½ oz. butter • 1 dessp. hot milk •

Arrange 12-14 paper baking cases on a baking sheet. Sieve flour, salt and sugar into a mixing bowl. Add fat all in one piece, eggs, milk and rind. Beat until smooth and creamy. Divide mixture evenly between the baking cases. Bake at Mark 4, 350 deg., for 20-25 minutes.
Make filling: Beat butter until soft, beat in half the sugar. Add hot milk and remainder of sugar, beat until smooth. When cakes are cool, cut off the tops and put a spoonful of butter cream in the centre of each. Cut the tops in half and replace as wings. Spread cream over join. Dust with icing sugar.

POLKA DOT DANDIES

You require: 4 oz. butter • 4 oz. castor sugar • 2 eggs • 4 oz. self-raising flour • 1 pkt. chocolate polka dots • 2 teasp. coffee essence • 10 oz. coffee flavoured butter cream •

Cream butter and sugar until very light. Add 2 lightly beaten eggs, one at a time, beating well between each. Add coffee essence. Fold in flour and chocolate dots, reserving a few for decoration. Spoon mixture into paper baking cases, which should be lightly dusted with flour. Bake at Mark 4, 350 deg., for 20 minutes. Cool, top each cake with coffee butter cream and a chocolate dot.

CHOCOLATE PALMIERS
Colour plate sixteen

You require: For pastry: 1 pkt. frozen puff pastry • 2 oz. castor sugar • For chocolate icing: 2 oz. plain chocolate • 1 tbsp. milk • 1 tbsp. water • 4 oz. sieved icing sugar • For filling: fresh whipped cream •

Roll out the pastry into a rectangle about 12 in. × 8 in. Sprinkle with castor sugar. Fold the lower and top edges over to meet in the centre. Press with a rolling pin. Repeat this process once more using remaining castor sugar. Brush the top with cold water and fold the two together to form a long sausage-shaped strip. Cut into ¼ in. slices. Place cut edge down on a baking sheet, allowing room to spread. Bake in oven Mark 7, 425 deg., until pale golden in colour. Cool on a wire tray. Make icing: Put the chocolate, milk and water into a basin over a pan of hot water. Allow to melt and then beat in the icing sugar. A little more water or sugar may be required to give a coating consistency.
Dip the ends of the palmiers into the chocolate icing. Allow to harden on a wire tray. Sandwich together with fresh whipped cream.

BRANDY SNAPS

You require: 2 oz. butter • 2 oz. castor sugar • 2 oz. black treacle • 1 teasp. lemon juice • 2 oz. plain flour • 1 level teasp. ground ginger • 2 oz. cream •

Melt butter, sugar, black treacle and lemon juice together over a gentle heat. Add sieved flour and ginger, blend together. Put teaspoonfuls of the mixture on well-greased baking trays, 5 in. apart. Bake 8-10 minutes at Mark 4, 350 deg., until a rich brown and well spread. Remove from the oven and leave to cool for a moment until they are easily lifted. While still warm, wrap each one around a wooden spoon handle, working quickly. Allow to become firm before lifting on to a wire tray. Store in an airtight tin, then serve filled with fresh cream.

To fill, whip the cream until stiff enough to pipe, and using an icing syringe or icing bag and a large rose tube, pipe a big rosette of cream into each end of the brandy snap.

Chocolate Palmiers

CHRISTMAS PUDDING CAKES

You require: 3 oz. super sifted self-raising flour • pinch salt • 2 oz. butter or margarine • 2 oz. castor sugar • 1½ oz. plain block chocolate • 1 egg • 1 dessp. milk • few drops vanilla essence • For icing: 4 oz. sieved icing sugar • 1 tbsp. warm water • yellow colouring • squeeze lemon juice • For decoration: holly leaves and berries made from almond paste, or artificial sprigs of holly •

Cut up chocolate and melt in a small saucepan in the milk. Cool. Cream the fat and sugar together. Beat in the egg gradually, adding a little of the

Brandy Snaps

Christmas Pudding Cakes

Place a group of 3 split almonds on top of each cake, in the centre of the whirl.

APRICOT BASKETS
Colour plate fifteen

You require: 3 oz. super sifted self-raising flour • pinch salt • 2 oz. butter or margarine • 2 oz. castor sugar • 1 egg • 1 dessp. milk • 3 drops vanilla essence • 5 fresh apricots or small can apricot halves • ¼ pkt. lemon jelly • just under ¼ pint syrup from can or water • ¼ pint double cream • piece of angelica 6 in. long •

Sieve flour and salt. Beat fat until soft, add sugar, beat again until light in colour and fluffy in texture. Beat in egg with a tablespoon of flour. Beat in milk, essence and more flour. Stir in rest of flour. Divide mixture evenly between 10 greased bun tins. Bake at Mark 5, 375 deg., for 15 minutes. Drain canned apricots or cook fresh ones gently in a little water and sugar, cut in half, remove stones. Dry fruit on a towel. Dissolve jelly in hot syrup or water to make ¼ pint. Cool until just starting to thicken. Arrange half an apricot on each cake, coat with jelly. Allow to set. Pipe small stars of whipped cream round the edges. Soak angelica in warm water until pliable. Cut

sieved flour and salt. Add the chocolate and vanilla essence. Stir in the remaining flour lightly but thoroughly. Half fill well-greased deep bun tins and bake at Mark 5, 375 deg., for 15-20 minutes.

Make icing: Put the sugar into a saucepan, add lemon juice. Add water very gradually and mix to a coating consistency. Add a few drops of yellow colouring, beat well. Stir over gentle heat for one minute. When the cakes are cold, put a small spoonful of icing on top of each, allowing to run down the sides. Decorate each cake with a small sprig of holly.

COFFEE ALMOND WHIRLS

You require: 4 oz. butter or margarine • 4 oz. castor sugar • 4 oz. self-raising flour • 2 heaped teasp. instant coffee • 2 eggs • 2 oz. split blanched almonds • pinch of salt • 12 oz. coffee butter icing •

Cream fat and sugar, gradually beat in eggs. Fold in sifted flour, coffee, salt, and all but a few of the nuts, finely chopped. Put heaped teaspoons of the mixture into floured paper cases and bake at Mark 5, 375 deg., for 20 minutes. Cool, and top each cake with a whirl of coffee butter icing.

Coffee Almond Whirls

Apricot Baskets

Chocolate Butterflies

Chocolate Palmiers

Chocolate Cream Shells

Dundee Cake

Glacé Fruit Cake and Cherry and Almond Cake

Rich Dark Fruit Cake

narrow strips and bend over baskets, pushing ends into cake to keep handles in position. If preferred, the fruit can be glazed with apricot jam instead of jelly. Heat 2 heaped tablespoons of jam with a tablespoon of water, strain, and use when cool.

ORANGES AND LEMONS

You require: For cakes: 2 eggs • 2 oz. castor sugar • orange essence • 1½ oz. self-raising flour • ½ oz. cocoa • 1 oz. melted margarine or butter • For decoration: 6 oz. icing sugar, approx. • orange colouring and essence • lemon colouring and essence • orange and lemon slices •

Line some patty tins with paper cake cases. Whisk the eggs, sugar and a few drops of orange essence together until thick, light and fluffy. Fold in the sieved flour and cocoa. Carefully stir in the melted margarine. Put spoonfuls of the mixture into the cake cases. Bake in oven mark 6, 400 deg., for about 10-15 minutes. Cool on a wire tray.

To decorate, make up a glacé icing using the icing sugar and a little water. Divide, and to one half of the icing add orange essence to taste and a few drops of orange colouring. Cover half the num-

ber of cakes and using orange slices, decorate as illustrated. To the remaining icing, add lemon essence and colouring. Cover the other cakes and decorate with lemon slices, from a box of sweets. Do not use fresh fruit.

Tested Tips

1. Small cakes are particularly liable to stick to their tins. Grease thoroughly the bottom of each bun tin, and if fancy moulded tins are used, into the grooves. When you remove the tins from the oven, loosen round the edges of each cake with the sharp point of a knife. After a minute, to allow the cakes to shrink away from the tins slightly, gently turn them out.

2. When filling paper cases, take care to put exactly the same amount of mixture into each case. To ensure this, you can place each case in the pan of your scales after filling and check that the weight is correct. Or use a spoon for filling which, when it is rounded, holds just enough for one cake. It is much harder to judge the quantity if you put several spoonfuls in each case.

Oranges and Lemons

Tuiles d'Amandes

MOCHA CREAM BUTTERFLIES

You require: For cakes: 3 oz. margarine • 3 oz. castor sugar • 1 egg • 4 oz. self-raising flour • 1 dessp. cocoa • teasp. instant coffee • For filling: butter cream or fresh cream •

Cream the fat and sugar until light and fluffy. Beat in the lightly whisked egg. Gradually fold in the sieved flour, coffee and cocoa, add warm water to form a stiff dropping consistency. Put 1 dessertspoon into each paper cake case. Bake at Mark 6, 400 deg., for 10-15 minutes. Allow to cool.

Using a sharp knife slice off the top of each cake and cut in half. Pipe the cream into the centre, arrange the wings. Dredge with icing sugar, if desired.

BUTTON RINGS

You require: For sponge: 3 eggs • 3 oz. castor sugar • 3 oz. self-raising flour • 1 level dessp. cocoa • For filling and decoration: Vanilla butter cream or whipped fresh cream • flaked almonds • sieved cocoa • chocolate buttons •

Grease and line a Swiss roll tin. Whisk the eggs

TUILES D'AMANDES

You require: 2 egg whites • 4 oz. castor sugar • 1½ oz. flour • 1 dessp. cocoa • ½ teasp. vanilla essence • 1 oz. flaked almonds • 2 oz. butter • For decoration: whipped fresh cream • mandarin oranges • cherries •

Whisk the egg whites and sugar together slightly. Stir in the sieved flour and cocoa, and the vanilla essence. Soften the butter and add, together with the flaked almonds, to the mixture. Place in small rounds, spreading with a teaspoon on to a greased baking tray. Space well. Bake at Mark 5, 375 deg., until firm, approx. 20 minutes depending on size. Loosen the biscuits from the tin and place them over a rolling pin, curling them round to form a 'U' shape. Do this quickly but firmly. Allow to cool before decorating.

To decorate, pipe the cream, using a large star tube and icing bag, down the centre of the biscuit. Decorate with fruit.

Mocha Cream Butterflies

66

and sugar together until light and fluffy. Carefully fold in the sieved flour and cocoa. Pour in to a Swiss roll tin and bake at Mark 5, 375 deg., for about 10-15 minutes. Turn on to a wire tray, remove the paper and allow to cool.

Using a plain cutter about 2 in. in diameter, cut the sponge into rings. Sandwich together in pairs with the cream. Spread a little around the sides of each cake and dip into flaked almonds. Cover the top with cream. Add sieved cocoa to the rest and using a small rose nozzle, decorate the edges with stars of chocolate cream. Complete decoration by adding a chocolate button to the centre of each.

Button Rings

FLORENTINES

You require: 3 oz. butter • 4 tbsp. milk • 4 oz. icing sugar • 1½ oz. flour • lemon juice • 5 oz. mixed dried fruit • 3 oz. flaked almonds • 2 oz. plain chocolate •

Melt the butter, milk and sugar in a pan – do not boil. Stir in the flour. Add the mixed fruit, nuts and a little lemon juice. Leave until cold. Spoon the mixture in small heaps on to a baking tray lined with rice paper, leaving plenty of room for the mixture to spread. Bake in oven Mark 5,

375 deg., for about 10 minutes. Allow to set. When cold, coat the underside with the chocolate. To do this, melt the chocolate over hot water. Put about a teaspoon on to the back of each biscuit. Complete decoration by making wavy lines on the chocolate with a fork.

When melting the chocolate, take great care not to keep it over the heat after it is melted, as this is inclined to cook the chocolate and cause it to lose its gloss. The water should be really hot but not boiling, and the basin in which the chocolate is melted should just touch the water.

Florentines

Chocolate Chip Butterscotch Brownies

SWISS TARTS

You require: 4 oz. butter • 1½ oz. icing sugar • 2 oz. flour • 2 oz. cornflour • jam or glacé icing •

Cream together butter and icing sugar. Work in flour and cornflour, then pipe into small paper cases. Bake for about 45 minutes at Mark 3, 335 deg., until pale brown. Fill centres with glacé icing or jam. Dust lightly with a little sieved icing sugar.

CHOCOLATE CHIP BUTTERSCOTCH BROWNIES

You require: For cakes: 4 oz. self-raising flour • pinch salt • 4 oz. butter or margarine • 2 oz. castor sugar •

Swiss Tarts

3 oz. black treacle • ½ teasp. vanilla essence • 2 eggs, beaten • 4 oz. chocolate chips • 2 oz. chopped nuts • For topping: 3 oz. butter • 4 oz. icing sugar • 1 oz. black treacle • chocolate chips •

Grease a 7 in. square tin. Sieve flour and salt. Melt butter in small saucepan, add sugar and black treacle and heat gently until sugar has dissolved. Pour into a bowl, add vanilla essence and beaten eggs. Beat for 1 minute. Blend in flour then fold in chocolate chips and nuts. Turn into prepared tin and bake in a moderate oven at Mark 4, 350 deg. Leave in tin to cool. When cold turn out. Cut in squares or fingers. Make up the topping by beating the sieved icing sugar, butter and black treacle together. Spread over the cake. Mark in a wavy pattern with the tines of a fork. Top each one with a diagonal row of three chocolate chips. If liked, spread the whole square of cake with the topping before cutting up, or to make a contrast, sprinkle some of the cakes thickly with icing sugar, and omit the topping.

CHOCOLATE BUTTERFLIES
Colour plate fifteen

You require: For cakes: 2 oz. super sifted self-raising flour • pinch salt • ½ oz. cocoa • 2 oz. butter or margarine • 2 oz. castor sugar • 1 egg • 1 tbsp. milk • 2 drops vanilla essence • For filling: 1½ oz. butter or margarine • 4 oz. icing sugar • 2 teasp. very hot milk • 2-3 drops vanilla essence •

Place 10 baking cases on a baking tray, or grease bun tins. Sieve flour, salt and cocoa. Beat fat until soft, add sugar, beat again until light in colour and fluffy in texture. Add egg with a tablespoon of flour, stir, then beat. Beat in milk, essence and a little more flour. Stir in rest of flour. Half fill cases or tins, smooth level. Bake at Mark 5, 375 deg., for 15-20 minutes.
Make filling: Beat fat until soft, add half sugar and beat very thoroughly. Add milk, rest of sugar and essence, beat until smooth. When cakes are cold, cut a round off the top of each. Put a spoonful of filling on each. Cut tops in half, place on the filling, rounded edges outwards. Dust with icing sugar.

Half Pound Cake

HOW TO MAKE AND COVER FRUIT CAKES

Fruit cakes can have a decorative finish, either baked with the cake (as for the Half Pound Cake shown in the photograph above) or put in position after it is cooked. Because they keep so well and become richer as they mature, fruit cakes are often used as the basis for elaborate iced and piped decorations. In this case they are coated with almond paste or fondant as a basis for the icing.

HALF POUND CAKE

You require: 8 oz. butter or margarine • 8 oz. castor sugar • 4 standard eggs • 8 oz. plain flour, sifted • 8 oz. mixed fruit, washed and dried • ½ oz. blanched almonds, cut into fine shreds •

Cream fat and sugar till light and fluffy. Beat in eggs one at a time, adding 1 tablespoon flour with each. Stir in fruit. Lastly, gently fold in remaining flour with a metal spoon. Turn mixture into a well-greased 1 lb. loaf tin. Sprinkle with almonds then bake in the centre of a warm oven at Mark 3, 335 deg., for 1½ hours.

CHERRY AND ALMOND CAKE
Colour plate seventeen

You require: ½ lb. self-raising flour • pinch salt • 4 oz. butter or margarine • 4 oz. sugar • 4 oz. chopped glacé cherries • 2 oz. chopped walnuts • 1 egg • 1 tbsp. golden syrup • 2-3 tbsp. milk • To decorate: little golden syrup • glacé cherries, halved • blanched almonds • angelica •

Sift the flour and salt into a basin. Add the butter or margarine and, with the fingertips, rub the fat in until the mixture resembles fine breadcrumbs. Stir in the sugar, glacé cherries, walnuts, beaten egg, golden syrup and the milk. Mix thoroughly. Pour the mixture into a greased, prepared loaf tin and bake in oven, Mark 5, 375 deg., for 20 minutes, reduce the heat to Mark 3, 335 deg., for a further 45 minutes. Remove cake from the oven. Turn out and immediately brush the top with a little golden syrup and then decorate with the halved glacé cherries and the angelica and

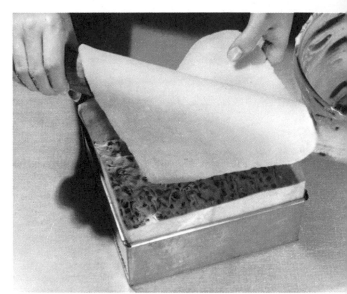

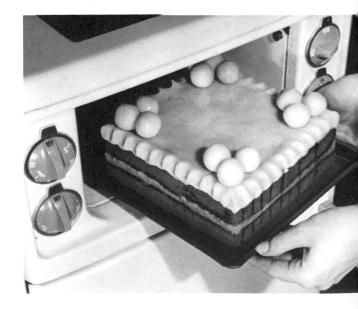

almonds to make a Christmas Tree as shown in the colour photograph.

GLACE FRUIT CAKE
Colour plate seventeen

You require: 5 oz. currants • 5 oz. seedless raisins • 6 oz. flour • pinch salt • ½ teasp. mixed spice • 5 oz. butter • 5 oz. soft brown sugar • 2 large eggs • 4 oz. chopped glacé cherries • 3 oz. blanched chopped almonds • grated rind and juice of 1 small lemon • 1 level tbsp. golden syrup • To decorate: glacé cherries • glacé pineapple • blanched almonds • raisins •

Prepare the fruit. Sift the flour, salt and spice together. Cream the butter and sugar together until soft. Add the eggs one at a time. Beat well. If the mixture starts to 'curdle' beat in a little flour. Fold in the flour mixture, dried fruits, glacé cherries, almonds, lemon juice and rind and the syrup. Spoon into a prepared 8 in. round cake tin, and bake in oven, Mark 1, 290 deg., for 3-3½ hours. Decorate as shown in colour plate.

SQUARE SIMNEL CAKE

You require: For cake: ½ lb. plain flour • pinch salt • 1 level teasp. mixed spice • ½ lb. butter or margarine • ½ lb. soft brown sugar • 4 large eggs • ½ lb. each, currants, sultanas and seedless raisins, washed and dried • 2 oz. glacé cherries, halved • 2 oz. mixed chopped peel • ¼ teasp. almond essence • finely grated rind of half an orange • apricot jam • For almond paste: 6 oz. castor sugar • 6 oz. icing sugar, sieved • 6 oz. ground almonds • 1 large egg • few drops each, almond and vanilla essences • sugar glaze •

Make almond paste: Mix together sugars and ground almonds. Form into a pliable paste with the egg and essences, then knead lightly till smooth and free from cracks.
Sift together, flour, salt and mixed spice. Cream fat and sugar till light and fluffy, then add the eggs one at a time, beating thoroughly after each addition. Add half the flour mixture then the fruit, cherries, peel, almond essence and orange rind. Stir in remaining flour and transfer half the mixture into a well-greased and lined 8 in. square cake tin. Cover with a third of the almond paste, rolled out on a lightly sugared board into an 8 in. square, then top with remaining cake mixture. Smooth with a palette knife. Bake cake in the centre of the oven at Mark 2, 310 deg., for 3-3½ hours. Leave in the tin for at least 10 minutes then turn out on to a wire tray. When completely cold, brush top with melted and sieved apricot jam and cover neatly with the second third of almond paste, pinching edges between the forefinger and thumb to give a decorative finish. Shape the remaining paste into twelve balls and put three in each corner, holding them in position with a little jam. Brush top of cake and balls with a syrup glaze made by briskly boiling together 2 tablespoons sugar and 2 tablespoons water for 3 minutes. Put cake under hot grill to toast lightly. Decorate with a posy of spring flowers.

ROUND SIMNEL CAKE

You require: For almond paste: ½ lb. ground almonds • 4 oz. castor sugar • 4 oz. icing sugar • juice of ½ lemon • ½ teasp. almond essence • 1 egg, beaten • For cake: 6 oz. plain flour • pinch salt • 1 teaspoon mixed spice • 4 oz. butter • 4 oz. castor sugar • 2 eggs • grated rind and juice of ½ lemon • ¾ lb. mixed dried fruits • 1 oz. candied peel • 1 oz. chopped blanched almonds, optional • warm redcurrant jelly • egg, optional •

Grease and line 6 in. round cake tin. Make almond paste: mix almonds, castor and sieved icing sugar

Round Simnel Cake

Stages in making a Simple Christmas Cake and preparing It for storage

together. Stir in lemon juice, almond essence and enough beaten egg to give a smooth, not sticky paste. Roll out about a third of almond paste into a 6 in. round.

Make cake: sift flour, salt and spice together. Cream butter and sugar. Beat in eggs, one at a time. Stir in lemon rind and juice. Fold in flour mixture then fruit, peel and almonds, if used. Put half of mixture in tin, level surface. Place almond paste round on top, pressing down firmly but gently. Put rest of cake mixture on top. Hollow out centre of cake. Bake at Mark 1, 290 deg., for 1 hour. Reduce heat to Mark ½, 265 deg., bake for further 3½-4 hours. Leave in tin for 5-10 minutes before turning out on to wire tray to cool.

Brush top of cake with redcurrant jelly. Roll out further third of almond paste to cover top of cake. Divide rest of almond paste into 11 pieces; roll each one into a ball. Place in ring on top of cake, securing with little redcurrant jelly. If liked, brush with little beaten egg and return to oven, Mark 7, 425 deg., for five minutes until lightly browned. When cold, decorate with tiny chicks or coloured sugar eggs.

The decoration formed by the eleven balls of almond paste is a traditional one. The number is significant, as it is intended to represent the number of apostles the twelfth – Judas – being omitted.

SIMPLE CHRISTMAS CAKE

You require: 12 oz. flour • pinch salt • 1½ teasp. mixed spice • 4 oz. almonds • 2¾ lb. mixed glacé cherries, chopped peel, chopped angelica and prepared mixed fruits, e.g. sultanas, currants, stoned raisins • grated rind and juice of 1 lemon • 8 oz. butter • 9 oz. soft brown sugar • 6 standard eggs • milk or brandy •

Line a 9 in. round or 8 in. square tin with two layers of greaseproof. Sieve dry ingredients. Blanch and chop almonds, cut cherries in half. Mix together chopped nuts, cherries, angelica, fruit, lemon juice and rind. In a large bowl, cream the butter and sugar together until a smooth and fluffy consistency. Beat in the eggs one at a time adding a level tablespoon of sifted flour if mixture curdles. Fold in the sieved flour, salt and spice, and enough milk or brandy to give a stiff dropping consistency. Add a few drops of gravy browning, if liked, to give a darker colour, then stir in the mixed fruit and nuts. Carefully spoon mixture into prepared tin and hollow out the centre. Bake at Mark 1, 290 deg., for 1 hour then reduce to Mark ½, 265 deg., for a further 4½-5 hours. When cold, pierce the base and sprinkle with 1-2 tablespoons brandy. Wrap in two layers of greaseproof and foil and store in a cool place till wanted.

Cover with almond paste at least four days before coating with icing, to prevent oil showing through.

Battenburg Cake

Preparing tins for fruit cakes

1. First prepare the base lining. Put the tin (either round or square) on top of 2 double thicknesses of greaseproof paper. Trace round the tin with a pencil and cut out on the inside of the pencilled tracing. Check to make sure the linings are an exact fit. Grease 3 of the circles or squares lightly, place on top of each other and cover with the fourth.

2. Now line the sides of the tin. For either round or square tins, take a length of 2 double thicknesses of greaseproof paper long enough to go round the tin and overlap by at least 1 inch, and deep enough to extend 2 inches above the rim of the tin. Grease 3 of the linings lightly, place on top of each other and cover with the fourth lining. Fold up 1 inch along the bottom, checking with a ruler that the fold is even all along, unfold and snip up to the fold marking at ½ in. intervals with a pair of scissors. Place inside the tin so that the cut ends overlap and the fold comes right to the bottom of the tin. Press in well, particularly into

the corners of square tins. Pin where the band overlaps and insert the base lining, pressing down to avoid trapped air. The tin is now ready to be filled with cake mixture. If the cake is very large, stand it on a wad of newspaper on the oven tray, and pin a layer of brown paper round the outside of the tin, to avoid burning.

BATTENBURG CAKE

You require: For cake: 6 oz. butter • 6 oz. castor sugar • 3 eggs • 8 oz. self-raising flour • vanilla essence • 1 tbsp. cocoa or cochineal and raspberry essence instead of cocoa for a pink and vanilla cake • For the filling and covering: 2 oz. butter or margarine • 4 oz. sieved icing sugar • vanilla essence • 1 tbsp. seedless or sieved jam • 6-8 oz. almond paste • little castor sugar •

Grease and line a 7 in. square cake tin. Fold a piece of greaseproof paper into several thicknesses and stand across the centre, dividing the tin into two equal parts. Cream the fat and sugar until light and fluffy. Beat in the whipped eggs a little at a time. Add the vanilla essence. Fold in the sieved flour, and enough water to form a soft dropping consistency. Turn half this mixture into one side of the tin. To the remaining mixture add the sieved cocoa, and a little more water if necessary to obtain a similar consistency. Turn into the other half of the tin. For a pink and vanilla cake, omit the vanilla essence and fold the sieved flour and enough water into the beaten mixture. Divide the mixture in two, add vanilla essence to one half and cochineal and raspberry essence to the other half. Turn into the two halves of the tin. Bake either cake at Mark 4, 350 deg., for about 50 minutes. Remove from the tin and cool on a wire tray.

Meanwhile prepare the butter cream by beating together the butter, icing sugar and vanilla essence and adding a little warm water to form a soft consistency. Trim the cakes and cut each into two even sized lengths. Sandwich together with butter cream, alternating the colours. Brush the long outside edges with jam. Roll the almond paste into a rectangle, large enough to completely cover the jammed sides. Roll the cake in this and seal the join well. Decorate the top with criss-cross scoring and flute the edges. Sprinkle with castor sugar.

NOVELTY SIMNEL CAKE

You require: For cake: 6 oz. butter • 6 oz. soft brown sugar • 3 eggs • 8 oz. flour • ½ teasp. ground cinnamon • ½ teasp. ground nutmeg • 1 dessp. cocoa • 4 oz. sultanas • 12 oz. currants • 2 oz. ground almonds • 1 lb. almond paste (Or 8 oz. ground almonds • 8 oz. icing or castor sugar • 1 egg • almond essence, if you prefer to make your own almond paste) • For decoration: sugar eggs • maidenhair fern • a little cocoa •

Make the almond paste in the usual way. Take one third and roll it into a circle to fit the cake tin. Cream the fat and sugar until light and fluffy. Beat in the eggs a little at a time. Carefully fold in the sieved flour, spices and cocoa. Stir in the prepared dried fruit and nuts. Put half the mixture into a greased and lined 7 in. cake tin. Cover with the round of almond paste. Put the remainder of the cake mixture on top and bake at Mark 4, 350 deg., for about 2½ hours. Allow to cool. Divide rest of almond paste into approximately half, cover the top of the cake with one piece. Roll a strip of the remaining almond paste to go round the edge of the cake and pinch the edge as shown in the picture. Decorate the top by dividing the rest of almond paste into approximately 13 small balls, place on top of cake and press a sugar egg into each ball, decorate with maidenhair fern. Dust 'eggs' lightly with a little cocoa through a sieve to represent speckles. For a children's Easter tea party, you could vary the decoration blending a little cocoa into the balls of almond paste for 'nests', and topping each with a fluffy yellow chick.

Novelty Simnel Cake

DUNDEE CAKE
Colour plate seventeen

You require: 8 oz. super sifted self-raising flour • a pinch mixed spice, optional • ¼ teasp. salt • 6 oz. butter • 6 oz. granulated or soft brown sugar • 3 eggs • 1 tbsp. milk • 2 oz. chopped peel • 6 oz. sultanas • 6 oz. currants • 1 oz. glacé cherries • 2 oz. blanched split almonds for the top •

Sieve flour, spice and salt. Beat butter until soft, add sugar, beat again until light and fluffy. Beat in eggs one at a time, together with a tablespoon flour, etc. Beat in milk and a little flour. Stir in fruit and rest of flour. Put mixture in a lined 7 in. round tin, arrange almonds on top. Bake at Mark 4, 350 deg., for 1 hour, then cover with paper and bake at Mark 2, 310 deg., for 1¼ hours.

RICH DARK FRUIT CAKE
Colour plate eighteen

You require: 1¾ lb. mixed dried fruit according to taste • ¼ teasp. salt • ¼ teasp. powdered nutmeg • 8 oz. butter • 6 oz. brown sugar • 3 eggs • rind of

Dundee Cake

one orange, grated • 1 tbsp. warmed syrup or treacle • 1 teasp. liquid browning • 6 tbsp. milk • ¾ lb. super sifted self-raising flour •

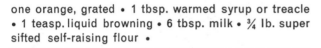

Prepare fruit, chopped cherries and large raisins if used. Sieve flour, salt and nutmeg. Beat butter until soft, add sugar, beat again until paler in colour and fluffy in texture. Beat in eggs, one at a time, together with a tablespoon of flour. Beat in orange rind, treacle, browning, half milk and a little more flour. Beat in rest of milk and a tablespoon flour. Stir in remainder of dry ingredients and fruit. Turn into a 9 in. round or 8 in. square tin, lined with double greaseproof paper, smooth level. Bake for 1 hour at Mark 4, 350 deg., then at Mark 1, 290 deg., for 1¾ hours. Leave in tin until cold, re-wrap in clean paper and a cloth, store.
If round cake is made, coat with almond paste as follows; if square, as described on page 77.

ALMOND PASTE

You require: ½ lb. icing sugar • 1 lb. ground almonds • ½ lb. castor sugar • 5-6 egg yolks or 2-3 lightly beaten eggs • few drops of almond essence to flavour •

Sieve the icing sugar and then mix thoroughly in a bowl with the ground almonds, essence and castor sugar. Add either the egg yolks or the lightly beaten eggs, and mix until it forms a smooth ball. Knead lightly with the fingertips.

To coat round cake: Trim the top of cake if it

is necessary, and then brush with warmed, sieved apricot jam. If the cake is not level, build up the edges with a small quantity of the almond paste until the top is even. Lightly dust a pastry board with sieved icing sugar. Take rather less than half of the almond paste, and carefully, but firmly, roll it out into a round to fit the top of the cake. Invert the cake on to the almond paste. Trim off the edges that show beneath the cake, then press down firmly. Lift up from the board. Roll out the remaining almond paste and divide into two.

Form each half into a strip which will fit the side of the cake. Trim. Now brush the two strips of paste with the warmed, sieved apricot jam, and apply to the sides of the cake by rolling it along the paste like a wheel. Smooth the joins at the side and top edge and then cover and leave to dry for at least 24 hours. Roll a jam jar round the sides to make smooth.

To coat square cake: Follow the same method for the top. Then for the sides, measure one side and cut 2 strips, each twice the length measured

and the correct depth. Use each strip to coat 2 sides of the cake, making the joins at opposite corners. Take care to make right angles at corners.

To prepare cakes for icing: Remember that it is much harder to correct faults in the shape of the cake with icing than when coating with almond paste, and make sure the cake is level on top, and a true circle or square. If uncertain whether the surface of the paste is still oily, brush with egg white or gelatine mixture.

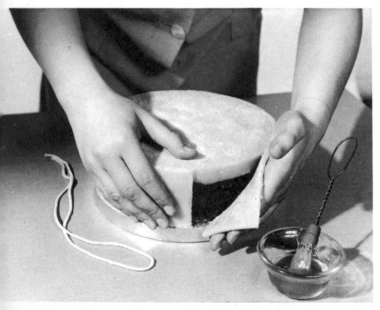

CHRISTMAS CAKE

You require: For cake: 11 oz. plain flour • ¼ teasp. salt • 1½ level teasp. mixed spice • 10 oz. butter • 10 oz. soft brown sugar • 5 eggs • 2 tbsp. black treacle • ½ teasp. vanilla essence • 2½ lb. mixed dried fruit • 5 oz. glacé cherries • 5 oz. glacé pineapple • 3 oz. chopped almonds • 3 tbsp. brandy or rum • For almond paste: 6 oz. castor sugar • 6 oz. icing sugar • 12 oz. ground almonds • 4 egg yolks • 3 tbsp. lemon juice • ¼ teasp. almond essence • For royal icing: 3 egg whites • 1½ lb. icing sugar • 1½ teasp. glycerine • 1 teasp. lemon juice •

Sift flour, salt and mixed spice. Cream fat and sugar till light and fluffy. Blend eggs with black treacle and vanilla essence. Beat in egg mixture a little at a time, sifting in one rounded tbsp. flour with each addition. Add dried fruit, glacé cherries, glacé pineapple and almonds, and mix thoroughly. Stir in remaining flour and transfer mixture to the 9 in. round cake tin, well greased and lined with a double thickness of greaseproof paper. Bake in the centre at Mark 3, 335 deg. for three hours, covering the cake with kitchen paper when it is nicely coloured. Leave at least 15 minutes before turning out on to a wire tray to cool. Wrap in greaseproof paper or aluminium foil and store in an airtight tin.

Note: The brandy or rum may be added to the mixture with the eggs, but it gives more flavour to the cake if the top is lightly pricked with a skewer and the spirit poured carefully over the cake the day before adding the almond paste.

Make almond paste: Mix sugars and ground almonds. Form into a pliable paste with the egg yolks beaten with lemon juice and essence. Knead lightly till smooth and free of cracks. Brush top and sides of cake with melted golden syrup or with two rounded tablespoons apricot jam, melted and sieved. Cover neatly with almond paste, then put cake aside in a cool place for 4 days to a week till the paste hardens.

Make royal icing: Lightly whisk egg whites, then add sugar a little at a time, beating well till icing is smooth and stiff enough to form small peaks. Stir in glycerine and lemon juice. Spread icing thickly over top and sides of cake, smoothing with a palette knife dipped from time to time in hot

water and shaken dry. Leave a few days for the icing to harden before decorating.

GOLDEN FRUIT CAKE
Colour plate three

You require: For cake: 6 oz. butter or margarine • 6 oz. castor sugar • 8 oz. plain flour • 1½ level teasp. baking powder • 3 eggs • 2 oz. desiccated coconut • 4 oz. sultanas • 6 oz. coarsely-chopped walnuts or Brazil nuts • 4 oz. well-drained chopped pineapple • 4 oz. mixed candied peel • 4 oz. chopped glacé cherries • little milk • For decoration: apricot jam, sieved • pineapple rings •

Cream together well the butter and sugar. Sieve dry ingredients. Gradually add the eggs to the butter or margarine, stir in the flour and all other ingredients, together with enough milk to give a soft mixture. Put into a 7-8 in. tin, lined with greased paper, and bake for 2½ hours in the centre of the oven. (Mark 3, 335 deg. for 1½ hours, then lower the heat slightly.)
Turn out and decorate. Brush top with sieved apricot jam and cover with a design in pineapple rings.

Brown Fruit Cake: Use brown sugar, drained chopped prunes or figs instead of pineapple, dark raisins instead of sultanas, and a little mixed spice to flavour.

Chocolate Fruit Cake: Use 2 oz. chocolate powder and 6 oz. flour instead of 8 oz. flour. Dust with sieved icing sugar or cover with chocolate icing and glacé fruits.

GOLDEN NUT RING

You require: 8 oz. margarine • 8 oz. castor sugar • 6 eggs yolks, or 3 large eggs • 10 oz. flour • 1 level teaspoon baking powder • 4 oz. chopped dates • 4 oz. chopped pecan nuts or walnuts • 4 oz. candied peel • 4 oz. glacé cherries • 4 oz. sultanas • 4 tbsp. milk • For decoration: 12 halved walnuts or pecan nuts • 4 glacé cherries • 4 strips candied peel •

Prepare a 9 in. ring tin or 8 in. round cake tin. Cream margarine and sugar until soft and light. Gradually add the eggs; if the mixture starts to curdle add a little flour. Fold in remaining sieved flour and baking powder, adding fruit, nuts, peel

and cherries. Lastly stir in milk. Put mixture into prepared tin and arrange nuts, cherries and peel on top. For a moist texture, tie a band of brown paper round the outside of the tin, deep enough to stand 1 in. above the rim. Bake in centre of the oven, Mark 3, 335 deg., for 1 hour, lowering temperature to Mark 1, 290 deg. for 1¼-1½ hours for ring cake and approximately 2-2¼ hours for the ordinary cake tin. The cake is cooked if it springs back when pressed lightly in the middle. It should shrink from the sides of the tin, and cannot be heard 'singing'. Do not turn out at once but leave until cool.

CANADIAN RING CAKE

You require: 8 oz. butter • 8 oz. castor sugar • 1½ level dessp. golden syrup • 4 eggs • 1 tbsp. milk • brandy or sherry • 8 oz. plain flour • 1 oz. ground almonds • grated rind 1 lemon and 1 orange • 1½ lb. white sultanas • 4 oz. chopped crystallized pineapple • 4 oz. chopped candied peel • 2-4 oz. blanched, finely chopped almonds, Brazils or hazel nuts • 2 oz. glacé cherries (quartered) •

Put the butter, sugar and syrup in a large mixing bowl. Cream until soft and light. Beat the eggs, milk, brandy or sherry and add very gradually to the butter mixture. If it shows signs of curdling, beat in a little flour. Fold in the flour and ground almonds, stir in the fruit, peel, nuts. Put into tin, prepared as previously described. Make sure the mixture is smooth on top. A 9 in. ring tin is suitable but you can use an 8 in. round or 7 in. square ordinary cake tin if you prefer. If using an ordinary cake tin, make a slight hollow in the centre to make sure the cooked cake will be flat on top. Bake ring cake in centre of oven for approximately 3 hours at Mark 3 or 335 deg. for the first hour, lowering temperature to Mark 2 or 310 deg. for rest of cooking time. If using an 8 in. round or 7 in. square ordinary tin, bake in centre of oven for about 3½ hours at same temperatures.

ROYAL ICING
AND PIPING TECHNIQUES

Very little special equipment is needed for icing and piping cakes, other than icing bags or syringes and a selection of tubes, or nozzles as they are sometimes described. Most kitchens contain such everyday items as basins, sieves, scissors, string, a pastry brush, spoons of various sizes, a spatula. You may have to invest in greaseproof and waxed paper, a paint brush and palette knife, wooden cocktail sticks for making flowers, and a fine skewer or large pin for marking designs. As time goes on, you will find it useful to have flat and serrated icing rulers, net nails for basket work, a cake marker, a pick board (instructions for making one are given on p. 93) and a turntable. Of these, only the last is fairly expensive, and it is worthwhile to buy a good one, as instead of constantly moving the cake to decorate different areas, you simply turn the table on which it stands.

Metal tubes are easily damaged. Never poke in a skewer to clear or clean them if blocked. Soak in very hot water or run hot water through them. All tubes and material icing bags as well as metal parts and syringes should be washed in very hot water, plastic parts in warm water. Dry thoroughly; metal (but not plastic) parts in a warm oven, bags by inverting over a milk bottle or jar in a warm place. Icing equipment should never be put away damp.

Coffee Engagement Cake

Child's Birthday Cake

Before the final coating of royal icing, a rich fruit cake must have some intermediate covering, to make the surface smooth and avoid lifting crumbs. While almond paste is the traditional choice, fondant icing is a useful alternative. This can in fact be itself decorated with piping, but it is usual to cover with royal icing before doing piped work.

FONDANT ICING

You require: 1 lb. icing sugar • 1 egg white • 2 fl. oz. liquid glucose • 1 teasp. almond essence •

Sieve the icing sugar twice, into a large basin. Make a well in the centre and add the egg white and glucose, with the almond essence. Beat the mixture steadily, gradually drawing in all the icing sugar. Turn on to a board dusted with icing sugar, knead until smooth and pliable. (Colouring can be added, if liked, at the kneading stage.) Roll out and apply to the cake by placing the whole piece on top of the cake. (First brush cake with egg white as a sealer.) Smooth down the sides, trimming away any surplus at the base.

CONDENSED MILK FONDANT ICING

You require: 1 lb. icing sugar • 2 tbsp. lemon juice • 4 tbsp. sweetened condensed milk •

Beat the sieved icing sugar into the sweetened condensed milk until smooth and creamy. Add the lemon juice and beat again. Use to cover cake, as for Fondant Icing.

Finishing a cake with royal icing

To demonstrate covering and decorating a cake with royal icing, stages in the process are shown in photographs on this and the following page. The finished cake, with bought decorations added, is the **Reindeer Christmas Cake** shown in colour plate twenty-seven.

Although royal icing is quite easy to make, there are several important points to watch. Whisk slowly and steadily for several minutes until mixture becomes very white and begins to stiffen. Beating too fast makes mixture appear stiffer than it really is. When icing is made, cover with a

Child's Birthday Cake

damp cloth and leave for at least an hour before using to allow air bubbles to subside, or they will mar the surface.

ROYAL ICING

You require: 4 egg whites • 2-2½ lb. icing sugar • 2 teasp. glycerine • (Leave the egg whites to stand overnight if possible – this makes for easier mixing. Remember to cover basin with a cloth.) •

Sieve icing sugar into a bowl. Stir about half of it, a little at a time, into the egg whites. Add glycerine. Beat well until smooth and glossy. Beat in enough of the remaining icing sugar for the icing to hold peaks. Place cake on turntable or on upturned plate. Spread approximately a third of icing over the top of the cake. Smooth icing in a band about ¾ -1 in. deep from the edge of the cake. Lift the icing in the centre of the cake in peaks – using just the tip of a round-bladed knife to do this. Spread most of the rest of the icing round sides of cake and put left-over icing in a basin. Cover with a piece of aluminium foil or polythene. Keep in a cool place and use for decorating. Using a palette knife or plastic scraper, smooth the sides of the cake. Hold palette knife or scraper upright and turn the turntable with the other hand. Allow the icing 1-2 days to dry out before the final decorating.

Fit a small rose tube into an icing bag and fill

with icing. Pipe a broad shell edge on top rim of cake, then pipe a second and third row on either side. Fit a shell tube into an icing bag and pipe a fine shell edge around the base of the cake. Leave to dry for 1-2 days before removing to a cake board or serving plate. Place decorations of your choice in position and hold in place with icing. Tie a red ribbon, if liked, round the side of the cake.

Quantities of royal icing to use

The given amounts of icing sugar that follow are enough for one layer to cover the cake and simple decorations.

7 in. round or 6 in. square cake: 1-1½ lb.
8 in. round or 7 in. square cake: 1½-1½ lb.
9 in. round or 8 in. square cake: 2-2½ lb.
10 in. round or 9 in. square cake: 2½-2½ lb.
11 in. round or 10 in. square cake: 2½-3 lb.

Metal syringes are very handy, especially when most of the decoration is being done with icing of one colour, and with only one or two different tubes. It is essential to fill them carefully, to avoid air locks in the icing. Spoon the icing into the body of the syringe, with the first tube you intend to use laid close by so that you can screw it in before the icing falls out. Make sure the icing goes in evenly, cutting across the surface with a knife if necessary to ensure that no air bubbles are trapped, until it is 1½ in. from the top. Insert the washer at an angle, sliding it down the side of the syringe. Now swing it into the upright position so that the washer slides home into the barrel. Press down lid and turn clockwise to lock. Press down plunger until icing appears, then screw in the first tube for use.

Polythene or material icing bags can be fitted with a screw top, which will take the same standard icing tubes as the metal syringe. These bags have the advantage of holding more icing for a large job, but the method of filling is different. Get the bag ready, with piping tube screwed in, drop gently into a jam jar taking care not to damage the tube; turn back one third of top of bag to keep edges clean and spoon in the icing, taking care again that there are no air locks, particularly at the narrow end of the bag. Screw the top just above the icing and exert pressure until it starts to appear from the tube.

Making and filling paper icing bags

Start with a 10 in. square of greaseproof paper. Cut in half diagonally to form two triangles. (Each triangle makes one bag.) Take one triangle and with the diagrams below in front of you, follow the steps from 1 to 7. It may help you to mark the three corners **A**, **B** and **C** the first time.

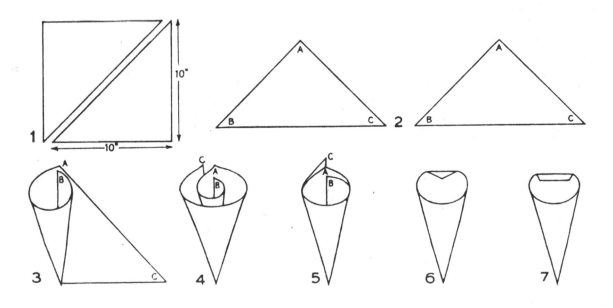

Fold corner **B** round inside corner **A**, and bring corner **C** round the outside of the bag, until it fits exactly behind **A**. All three corners must be together, and the point of the bag neatly closed. Fold corner **A** over two or three times to hold the bag together. Snip a small piece off the point for piping, or cut off a large end, about ½ in. up from the tip, and drop in a fancy tube.

Remember that paper forcing bags are fragile, and useful mainly for small icing jobs, or where you need to switch from one colour to another, or one tube to another, frequently. A larger bag which would hold more icing would only tend to split from the greater pressure of the contents and the heat and moisture of your hand. To fill the bag, spoon in the icing until half full, and fold top over about ½ in. Fold over again until close to contents, then fold the two tips inwards towards the centre, and press with your right thumb on the join to force out the icing. The fingers should be spread out loosely supporting and directing the bag, and the left hand used under the right hand as an additional support.

Another icing which can be used as a basis for decorations in royal icing is flat icing. And there is yet another type, satin icing paste, which can be used as a covering and for moulded decorations.

FLAT ICING

You require: 1¼ lb. icing sugar • 2 large egg whites • 1 teasp. almond essence • colouring

Sieve the icing sugar twice, and bind to a stiff paste with the unbeaten egg whites. Knead on a board dusted with icing sugar until quite smooth. Colouring and essence can be added at the kneading stage. To cover a cake, divide icing in half, knead one half into a smooth ball, and roll into a circle or shape into a square to fit the top of the cake exactly. Divide remainder and roll each ball into a strip to fit half way round the sides of the cake.

SATIN ICING PASTE

You require: 12 oz. icing sugar • 1 oz. table margarine • 2 tbsp. lemon juice •

Melt the table margarine with the lemon juice in a medium-sized saucepan over a low heat. It should never become hotter than blood heat. (Colouring can be added at this stage if required.) Stir in 4 oz. sieved icing sugar, return pan to a very low heat until the sugar is dissolved and bubbles begin to form at the side of the pan. Then continue cooking for only 2 minutes. Time carefully, as icing may crystallize if overboiled. Remove from heat and gradually stir in remaining icing sugar. Beat well with a wooden spoon until cool. Knead well on a board dusted with icing sugar, adding more sieved icing sugar if needed to make a smooth, pliable mixture, which will become whiter the longer it is kneaded. Use immediately or wrap in greaseproof paper and store in a polythene bag in a cool, dry place. Knead again just before using.

Various finishes using a cake ruler

A cake ruler can be used for making a really flat surface for decorating, as shown on page 84, or for making an interesting grooved finish by using the serrated edge. To finish the top of the cake, hold the ruler lightly by the two ends well clear of the cake and draw it across the top of the cake towards you, so that it skims off any surplus icing. For a grooved surface now reverse the ruler and repeat the process with the serrated side.

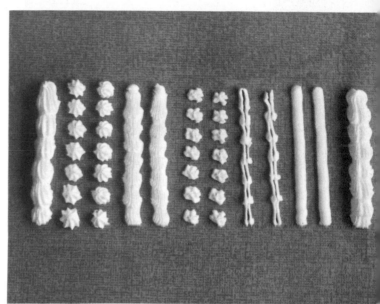

First steps in decorating

Using a writing tube requires confidence. Write your greeting on greaseproof paper, ruling a straight line or parallel lines to help you, and measuring just how many inches you have to fill. Use either roman capitals or ordinary handwriting as shown here but remember joined writing is more difficult, as you cannot pause and rest after each letter. Prick out the writing through the paper on to the cake with a large pin, and ice over the holes, being careful to cover them.

The use of other tubes is shown right, for shell edgings, borders, stars and rosettes. The outer borders are made with number 21, 12-star tube, then come two lines each of number 23, wide raised band tube; number 16, double thread tube; number 31, clematis tube; number 12, shell tube; number 8, 8-star tube. Over-piping, also shown right, is used to build up decorations to give them

85

by over-piping twice, each time using a finer tube and usually finishing with a number 1 writer. Borders can be over-piped with a heavier tube, and often help to disguise irregular edges. An example is given here in stages, showing how a design is built up, using a Tala cake marker to simplify the marking out, and using piped baskets as decoration.

How to use a cake marker

It is made from 2 wedge-shaped pieces of plastic, hinged together. Their common pivot is pierced so that the marker can be fixed in position with a pin. One of the wedges is pierced at equal distances with holes large enough to put a pin or pencil through. One wedge equals one-sixteenth of a circle, but the two wedges can be hinged together to form one-eighth, one-tenth, or one-twelfth of a circle, and cake tops divided up accordingly. First find the centre of the cake. Open the marker so that the centre lines of the two wedges form one straight line across. Place on top of cake and move about until the wedge ends are at equal distances from the cake edge. Fix pivot in position with a pin as shown. Now mark concentric circles by inserting a pencil in any hole in the wedge and swivelling it round until the circle is complete. Wedge shaped sections can be made by using one part of the marker, or the two wedges hinged together, and marking close to the sides of the wedge. Scrolls can be pricked in through the marker, also loops and garlands using the marker to indicate the ends and deepest central point. In the

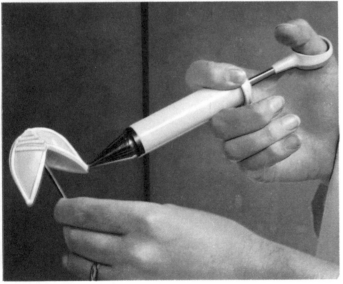

more importance. If you have made a border of coiled shell edging, you can overpipe with a writing tube in the same or a contrasting colour with lines or dots, to give a much more sharply defined raised effect. Coiled shell edgings and over-piping are demonstrated in the Christening Cake designs on pages 104 and 105.

Always be careful to use a tube of smaller diameter than the first, or the effect will be clumsy. If the icing is allowed to dry completely between each application, a most professional finish can be given

Stages of Basket Cake

Finished cake trimmed with baskets

following pages you will see how to prepare and carry out a number of designs using the cake marker, or paper patterns (usually called templates).

How to decorate a cake with baskets

Place the plain-iced cake on a board 2 in. larger in circumference, and cover out to edge of board with icing. Using the cake marker, divide the top of the cake into 16 sections. Mark dots on the cake using holes number $4\frac{1}{2}$, $3\frac{1}{2}$, 3, $2\frac{1}{2}$. Draw convex semi-circles by joining holes $4\frac{1}{2}$ and $3\frac{1}{2}$. Draw concave semi-circles by joining holes 3 and $2\frac{1}{2}$. Mark dots on cake at 4 opposite points using hole number $1\frac{1}{2}$. Finally, draw a square by joining the 4 dots. Compare the result with the photograph shown top left on p. 86, to make sure that your design has been carried out correctly.

Make some half border moulds (for which the method is fully described overleaf). In case some are spoiled, it would be wiser to make about 10, although only 8 are required for the cake. You will need border net nails and a number 2 writer tube for these, and an icing pen as shown here (which is really only a smaller and lighter form of the icing syringe) or a small paper forcing bag. In this simple type of basket only half the net nail is covered, and is easy to remove from the nail without breaking. Now begin the decoration. Using a number 2 writer tube, fill in the square with rows of parallel lines, $\frac{1}{2}$ in. apart, then cross with another similar set of parallel lines at right angles. You will have little difficulty keeping the trellis-work even as the area to be covered is not large. When dry, over-pipe a border with tube number 6 to outline the square. Pipe in the concave and convex semicircles with number 3 writer tube. (By working from the centre outwards you avoid damaging the completed piping.) Decorate round the top and base of the cake, using tube number 5, with a wavy action. Edge the rim of the board with tiny shells using tube number 3. Attach the half-border moulds to the sides of the cake with a little icing, using tube number 3, and placing the open point of the basket directly under the join of two adjacent convex semi-circles. Although at first glance these directions sound

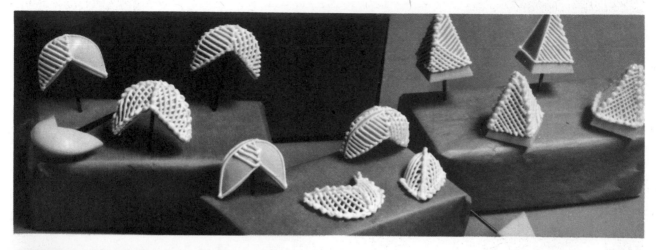

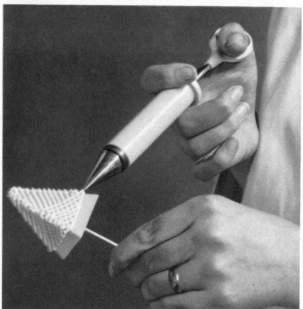

rather like a lesson in geometry, they are really easy to follow if you consult the photographs frequently.

How to make raised trellis baskets

The net nails already referred to are moulds of various shapes, mounted on a pointed stem. Before use, the mould should always be slightly greased with lard or cooking fat. You have the choice of 3 shapes – the oval (or basket), the pyramid, and the border. You can see above the various stages of covering an oval net nail completely, to fit over the top and side of a cake, of half-covering; also demonstrated are stages in completely covering a pyramid net nail. If only two sides of the pyramid are covered, it can be affixed to the side of a cake rather like a wall-vase. The size can be varied by carrying the trellis right to the base of the nail or by ending it two-thirds of the way down, as shown left. This photograph also shows you how easy it is to hold the nail in your left hand and pipe with the right hand, turning the nail when required.

If you are short of nails, make two baskets on each nail at the same time, making sure that the icing is separated, and you can then remove two baskets from each nail. As each basket is completed, press the point of the nail into a sheet of thick cork, or through the shallow lid of a cardboard box and forty-eight hours later they will be hard and firm. The baskets can be eased gently off the moulds with the point of a knife if the air is

Twenty-first Birthday Cake

Perfection Wedding Cake

Sweethearts' Wedding Cake

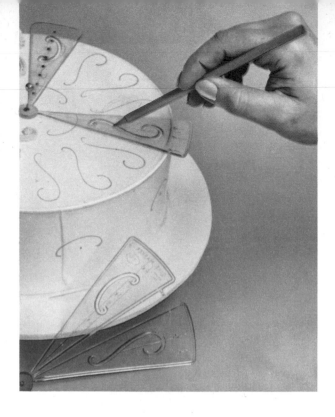

warm; if they stick, place them near a fire or other source of heat to warm through. Note that the baskets will be less liable to break if all the seams are over-piped in some decorative way, and that this will increase the weight of the basket. Therefore when fixing (especially to the side of the cake) anchor with pins driven through the basket into the cake to take the weight until dry.

Contrast Panels. Another form of decoration which can be used with or without basket work, is achieved by outlined panels – round, oval medallions, or square – with rosettes and filling (or flooding) with rather runny icing of a contrasting colour. See how to do it in the photograph on page 88.

How to decorate a cake with scrolls

Put the plain-iced cake on a board 2 in. larger in circumference, and cover out to edge of board with icing. Using the cake marker, divide the top of the cake into 16 sections. Then using the "S" scroll, draw lightly with a pencil 16 scrolls, one in each section. Turn the plastic wedge over each time, so that alternate scrolls face opposite ways. Using the "C" scroll, draw 4 scrolls in the centre of the cake evenly spaced out round it. Draw in 8 "C" scrolls on the sides of the cake, centring each one under a facing pair of "S" scrolls on top. Now consult the photographs to make sure that you have carried out the design correctly; then begin the decoration. Using number 8 star tube, and icing tinted a pastel shade to contrast with the white background, pipe in all the "S" scrolls, and the centre rosette. Use number 20 fine rope tube to pipe in all the "C" scrolls. Make a shell border round the top edge of the cake, using number 5 rope tube. (Make sure the side scrolls are dry before doing this, or leave piping them until after the top edging.) Make dots on the sides using number 3 writer in between the "C" scrolls, graduating in size by the amount of icing used. Make a border round the base of the cake with tube number 20, using a wavy action. Pipe tiny shells round edge of board with tube number 20. (Note that in these as in other designs, it is not essential to use exactly the tubes recommended. By using other, slightly different, tubes you happen to have available, you will get roughly

Scroll Cake

89

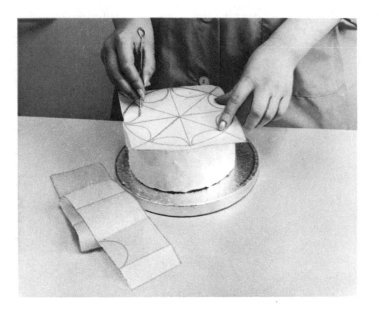
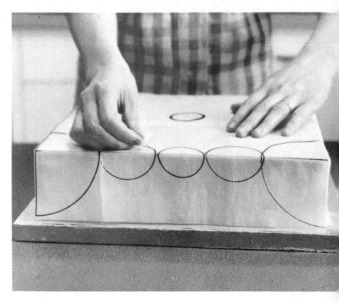

the same effect, but will add an individual touch of your own to the design.)

Although most methods of using tubes to produce different effects will be explained as they occur, when following recipes from other sources it may be useful to understand certain terms such as scrolling or coiling, and doubling. The former is done by moving the tube in close, anti-clockwise "e" shapes; the latter by checking the flow of icing with a slight backwards movement every inch or half-inch. Shaking means using a wavy movement, as shown on page 89.

How to create your own designs

By making your own paper pattern or template, you can create your own personal designs and express your own ideas freely. You will need greaseproof paper, pencil, scissors, and a pin. You will also need saucers, cups and glasses of different sizes for curved patterns.

Round Cake Designing. Cut a square of greaseproof paper just large enough to cover the top of the cake. Either trim, using cake tin as a guide, or leave the corners to assist you in moving the pattern about on top of the cake. Draw a circle round the tin on the paper. Fold it diagonally both ways to find the centre, mark with pencil, and smooth out pattern. Measure and mark cen-

tres of all four sides, join opposite points. The top of the pattern is now divided into 8 equal wedges. A simple loop in each section can be drawn round a glass, as shown above, but you can draw round a diamond shape cut from cardboard, or have different patterns in alternate sections – the choice is endless. Fix the centre of the pattern carefully to the cake with a pin, so that it fits exactly, and prick out the design, clearly and close enough so that it will be easily visible when you remove the pattern. Now make the side template. Measure the circumference of the cake with a piece of string, cut a strip of greaseproof paper exactly the same depth as the cake and the same length as the string plus $\frac{1}{2}$ in. Ignoring the extra $\frac{1}{2}$ in. (used for pinning round cake as an overlap), fold paper in half, in quarters, then in eighths. Spread out and you will have 8 equal section marked by creases. Pencil them in, and either repeat the design used on top of the cake, or a new one, perhaps a pretty shape you can fill in with massed rosettes. Pin pattern round cake and prick through.

Square Cake Designing. Although this sounds hard, it is really easier still, as the design can be planned to fit the top and one side together on a single piece of paper, and the pattern turned until all the four sides have been pricked through it. The finished cake is shown in colour plate 25.

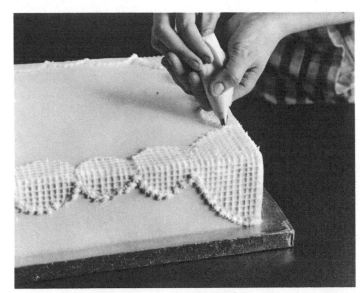

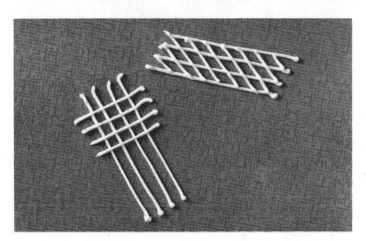

This is a really large cake, baked in a square 11 in. tin, and measuring 12 in. square when covered with almond paste and plain royal icing. A pattern was cut 15 in. × 12 in. for the top and a 3 in. side. A line was drawn across to mark the division between top and side, leaving a 12 in. square and 3 in. × 12 in. strip. A saucer measuring 5 in. across was used to draw rather more than half a full circle which cut the line $2\frac{3}{4}$ in. in from the edge. The centre of the line was marked (by measuring 6 in. along from one end) and a small wineglass was used to draw a circle 2 in. across, centred on this point and half on the top, half on the side of the pattern. A slightly larger glass was used to make circles on either side of this $2\frac{1}{4}$ in. across. The centre of the top of the pattern was marked with a circle. The design was then pricked out through it.

Piping the Lucky Horseshoe Cake. Using the right-angled corners of the cake as a guide, the top and side semi-circles and fan shapes were piped in, using a number 2 writer tube and square trellis. The difference between this and diamond trellis is demonstrated in the photograph above right. Tiny stars were piped to outline the edges of the trellis and the sides and corners of the cake, disguising any irregularities, with a number 6 fine star tube. A group of stars was piped at the base

in the centre of each side and an ornament placed against the front group. Holes were made in the centre of each corner fan on top with a fine skewer so that ornaments could be pushed in and the central horseshoe placed in position.

Decorating the Rose Garland Cake

Put the plain-iced cake on a board 2 in. larger in circumference, and cover out to edge of board with icing. Tint some icing red and some green, and make about 4 dozen sugar roses and about twice as many leaves, as described in the following chapter. Divide top of cake into 16 with cake marker as previously described, and use number 2 writer tube to mark out the concave and convex semi–circles, doubling the tube for a fancy effect. Use number 11 tube to make wavy border to top edge of cake. Use number 19 tube, doubling to give a wavy effect, to make slanting lines round the sides of the cake. Each one begins at one of the 8 centre dividers, and finishes directly beneath the next one. Pipe a maze border with the finest writer tube you have out to the edge of the board. Pipe a shell border round the base of the cake with tube number 20, and with the same tube, a border of much smaller shells round the edge of the board. Put the roses in position as shown in the photograph above and two leaves on either side of each one, using tiny dabs of icing. If preferred, the roses and leaves could be white.

MAKING SEPARATE SUGAR DECORATIONS BY AUDREY ELLIS

Besides the decorations which are piped straight on to the cake itself, there are others which can be made separately, dried off, and then attached to the cake with icing. Of these, the easiest and prettiest you can make are piped sugar flowers. They are best made of royal icing, well beaten so that the icing stands in peaks in the mixing bowl when lifted with a spoon. A few drops of acetic acid should be added as this makes the icing set more firmly and, if required, food colourings to tint the icing to the appropriate shade for the flower you are copying. According to the size of flower you want, use Nos. 11 or 42 flat petal tubes, or for roses, Nos. 18 or 36 curved petal tubes. Raised flowers are piped on to a pick, which is removed when they are dry: flat flowers are piped on to waxed paper, and eased off with a palette knife when dry. Of the raised flowers, roses are the most popular.

How to pipe sugar roses

To make the wooden picks on which sugar flowers are piped, trim one pointed end off a wooden cocktail stick with a sharp knife, leaving the stick about 2 in. long. The blunt end passes through a hole in the pick board and rests on the table top. Children's games sometimes include a pick board for scoring, but if you have to make one, by far the easiest method is to cut a piece of pegboard about 8 in. × 12 in. and nail two 1 in. wooden battens down the short sides, or support it during use on two books of even thickness, placed under opposite ends.

You will also find it useful to have a piece of thick cardboard about 6 in. × 8 in. with a 2 in. slit, about ¼ in. wide, cut in one of the long sides. To remove sugar flowers from picks, you slide the pick along the slit, and remove the pick downwards, leaving the sugar flower resting on the cardboard, where you can easily slip it off on to a sheet of greaseproof paper.

Make up a small batch of royal icing as described opposite and if liked, tint pink. To make them more realistic, have two batches of icing and two piping bags, with different shades of icing. For instance, use deep pink for the centre of the roses,

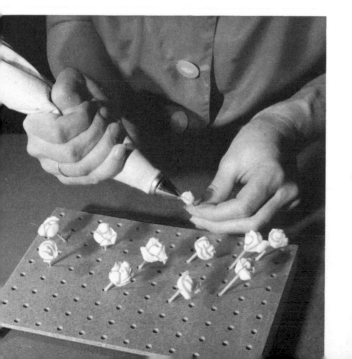
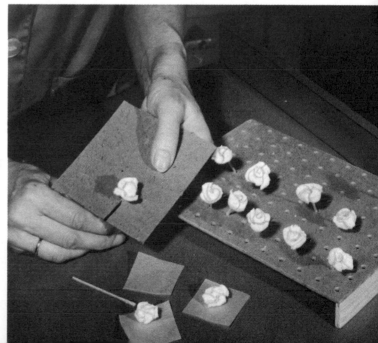

Cadbury Bros.

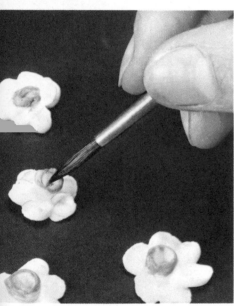

ping a new petal over the last one, and turning the stick to get a free, easy movement. When the flower looks large enough, put the stick holding it into the pick board so that it rests holding the flower clear of the board. If the flower seems top-heavy on one side, you can slant the pick to correct this till it dries. When the flowers are quite dry (overnight if possible) remove on to greaseproof paper by running the stick down the slit in a piece of cardboard, as described on page 93 and easing out the stick. The rose will be left resting on the cardboard; slide it carefully on to a sheet of greaseproof paper so as not to damage it. Make as many roses as you require for the decoration, which you will have planned out in advance, and make a few extras to allow for breakages in handling. If the design calls for some buds, finish them off without adding the five open petals.

Flat piped flowers are easier to make, if rather less effective than roses.

How to pipe sugar narcissi

Work each flower individually on a small square of waxed paper fixed on to an icing nail. The nails have plastic heads about twice the size of a drawing pin, fixed to a spike like a thin skewer. While piping fix the waxed paper to the head of the nail with a dab of icing. Again, use stiff royal icing with a drop or two of acetic acid added. Using a small petal tube and plain white icing, pipe the first petal using a semi-circular movement, turn-

and pale pink for the outer petals. Hold the small stick or pick in your left hand with the tube held against the upper end of the stick, and pipe round it three times to form the centre of the rose. Practise twirling the stick in the opposite direction as you force out the icing until you get the 'feel' of this movement. Now make three fairly tight petals round the bud. Beginning each time at the base, pipe a semi-circle of icing, finishing off the petal and beginning the next overlapping it as you turn the stick. (If using two shades of icing, change to the lighter shade now.) Pipe three to five more petals, with a more open movement so that the edges turn back more, always overlap-

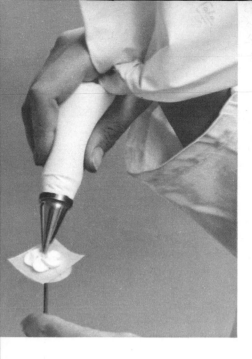

British Sugar Corporation

ing the icing nail slowly in the opposite direction. Pipe six petals altogether to complete the circle of the flower. After three petals have been piped, an exact half-circle should have been made. Now pipe a complete circle on top of the petals to form the centre of the flower. Make as many as required plus a few spares. Allow the flowers to dry completely before removing from the paper. When dry, paint the centres yellow with a clean paint brush and saffron food colouring. Use the end of a palette knife (heated if you experience difficulty) to remove flowers. Lift into position on cake with tweezers, taking care not to crush them. Very simple flat flowers with four, five or more

petals look quite effective done in any delicate pastel colour, provided the petals are all piped in neatly to the centre. The flowers can be placed in groups of three, or used as a wreath border to a square or circle filled in with piped trellis work, or to surround medallions on the side of a cake.

How to make moulded roses

Quite large and most realistic flowers, especially roses, can be moulded from almond paste, or Satin Icing Paste. Begin by working sufficient food colouring into the paste to colour as required. Knead the paste until the colour is evenly

Six stages in moulding a rose from almond paste, actual size

Cadbury Bros.

Colman's Fine Semolina

1 lb. loaf sugar • ¼ pint water • large pinch cream of tartar • 4 oz. fine semolina • 8 oz. ground almonds • 2 egg whites, lightly beaten • few drops each almond and vanilla essence • 4 oz. sieved icing sugar •

Slowly dissolve loaf sugar in water. Add cream of tartar. Bring to boil and boil till mixture forms a soft ball when dropped in cold water (240° F., if using a sugar thermometer). Remove from heat and stir briskly till syrup becomes grainy and opaque. Beat in fine semolina, almonds, egg whites and flavourings, then work in sieved icing sugar. Knead on a slab or board, dusted with sieved icing sugar till smooth and cold. Colour and mould into fruits as required. When dry, paint with edible food colourings if necessary.

Raspberries: Tint some of the paste deep pink. Tint a very small quantity bright green. Form tiny balls of the pink paste into the shape of a raspberry, mark all over with the point of fine skewer. Roll tiny spikes of green paste and press into base of fruit, at stalk end.

Oranges and lemons: Tint some of the paste orange and some yellow. Form the orange paste into round balls, mark all over close together lightly with skewer and indent deeply at one end. Form the yellow paste into slightly more oval shapes for lemons, and finish as for oranges. Paint in stalk end with green food colouring.

Pears: Tint some of the paste very pale green and form into tiny pear shapes. Trim cloves to make suitable sized stalk and base for pears. If liked, paint one side of the pears with pink food colouring to imitate the skins of ripe pears.

Bananas: Tint some of the paste yellow. Form into tiny banana shapes, making one flat side, and two parallel ridges on top coming together at each end of the fruit. Paint in lines along these ridges with brown food colouring and dots at either end.

distributed. Following the stages shown in the photograph on the previous pages begin by working a small piece of paste with the fingers until it is a suitable petal shape. Roll to make centre of the rose. To make the rest of the petals, work the paste into thin rose-petal shapes as for the first petal. Place one petal on either side of the moulded centre, furling closely round it. Work five more petals and overlap round the other two. The completed rose should have seven overlapping petals. Cut off any excess paste at the base with a pair of scissors. Allow to dry thoroughly on a piece of waxed paper before placing them in position on the cake. If you would like to add leaves and stems to your roses, tint some of the paste with sap green colouring. Roll out thinly. Cut a strip with a curved inner edge and the outer edge cut in five sharp points for the calyx. Wrap round the base of the rose, and turn back the points slightly. Using a real rose leaf (or picture) as guide for shape, cut out leaves in proportion to the size of your moulded flowers. Mark in the veins and serrate the edges. Roll out thin 'ropes' of paste for stalks.

Another really effective form of decoration can be made by moulding fruit, or even vegetables, from almond paste.

If preferred, fruits (and vegetables) can be moulded from almond paste, and then painted with food colourings, instead of kneading the colourings into the paste. If you enjoy painting, this delicate work can be more interesting. Do not aim to get all

Lucky Horseshoe Wedding Cake

Joy's Easter Nest

*Snow Peak Christmas Cake
and Golden Bauble Christmas Cake*

the items in true relation to their natural sizes (for example, a marzipan orange much larger than the raspberry) but roughly all the same size. When moulding vegetables it is a convention to show half a split pea pod with the peas resting in this open half. Potatoes are moulded as roughly shaped balls with a few indentations only, then rolled in cocoa.

Another form of decoration is the run-in 'plaque', or flat shape specially useful for applying to the sides of a cake.

How to make plaques

They are usually made in a colour that contrasts with the icing of the cake so that it shows up well. There are several ways of making these, but the simplest way for the beginner is to draw round the shape of a fancy cutter on white card. For a child's party cake, animal cutters would be particularly suitable.

We show four easily recognized shapes, a duck, a dog, a rabbit and bear. A sheet of waxed paper twice the width of the card on which the shapes have been drawn is laid over it, so that the upper left hand corners of both card and waxed paper match. The paper is anchored to the card by four tiny dabs of icing. Now, using a No. 1 writing pipe and fairly firm glacé icing tinted the required colour, pipe over the outlines of the animals. While these dry, slide the paper across, anchor again with icing, and trace out another set of animals. (You will now have a set of eight tracings.) Thin the icing slightly, so that it will flow readily, and using a large tube or grease-proof paper bag with a small diagonal snipped off the end, fill in the whole outline. This process is called 'flooding'. Use the rounded blade of a knife or a blunt skewer to help the icing into the corners of the pattern, taking care not to overrun the edge. Allow to dry out at least overnight, or longer. Now with a No. 1 writing tube, pipe in any details you wish, such as dots for the eyes, a collar for the dog, etc., and leave again to dry. With scissors, cut into squares each containing one animal. To remove from the paper, place the square of paper close to and parallel with the edge of the table. Slide out paper over edge until

one-third of animal protrudes past edge of table, begin to peel back the paper under it, supporting the body of the plaque flat on the table with the fingers of the other hand. Gradually ease paper away until half the animal is released, reverse so that free side is resting on table with paper pressed back against edge. Ease this half of the paper away, sliding plaque back on to table-top as you do this. (If set really hard before the paper is removed, there is little danger of the plaques breaking, but do not be tempted to try it too soon).

After some experience you can attempt quite complicated designs. For example figures of children, circus animals and clowns, or fairytale characters, can be traced from a book on to white card, the outlines piped over this, then flooded, and the details copied with a No. 1 writing tube and different coloured icings.

The type of almond paste recommended for moulding fruits, and also stiff Satin Icing Paste, are suitable for patchwork icing.

How to make patchwork icing

Use an embroidery transfer with a central figure, or perhaps a cottage, for the top of the cake, and smaller details of the transfer such as flowers or small animals to go round the sides. Tint the almond paste at least four different colours, such as pink (for faces and hands) brown (for hair, shoes, etc.) and two bright colours for clothing. If a cottage scene is chosen you will need brown for roof, fence, etc., green for foliage, and two pastel shades for flowers. Roll out each piece of paste very thinly. Cut up the transfer, place each piece pattern-wise on the appropriate coloured paste and cut round it with a sharp knife. (Keep board, rolling pin and hands lightly dusted

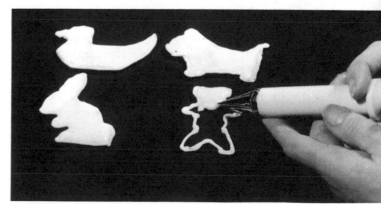

British Sugar Corporation

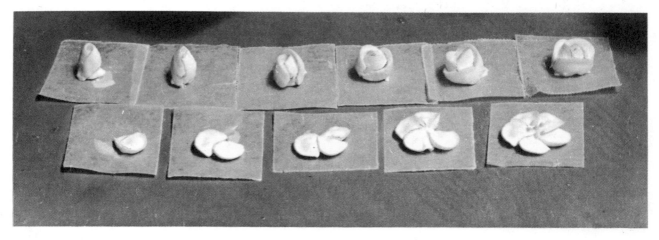

Different ways to pipe raised and flat flowers

with cornflour during the process.) Brush surface of icing with a thin layer of egg white, and assemble the pieces of the pattern. Allow to dry off overnight. With a fine paint brush and brown food colouring, paint in details, such a features on faces and folds of clothing, panes in cottage windows. Piped two-toned flowers can be worked into these designs and are realistic.

How to make two-toned flowers

Raised flowers piped round picks or flat-piped on waxed paper can be given shaped petals. To make pansies, fill the syringe or icing bag with a large spoonful of yellow tinted icing placed in one side, and a large spoonful of mauve tinted icing in the other. As you adjust the plunger or turn down the top of the bag, the two lots of icing will come together, and after testing to make sure both colours are flowing out of the tube, you can flat-pipe the pansies, using the same methods as for narcissi, making five petals only. When the flowers are dry, pipe a group of dots in the centre, with icing tinted a stronger shade of yellow, and a No. 1 writing tube, and draw out a few short lines with brown food colouring and a fine paint brush a little way from the centre to edge. To make a wild rose, line the icing bag with white icing and fill centre with pale pink icing, make five petals and finish with yellow centres as for pansies.

Leaves to go with piped flowers can also be piped out flat on to waxed paper with icing tinted green and leaf tube No. 17, or No. 10 for larger leaves. Draw the point of the tube away sharply to make raised leaves. Pipe plenty so you need only use the best shaped ones.

Bought cake decorations

The most useful are silver dragees in the shape of balls, to place on piped rosettes elaborating simple decorative piping, or closed together in rows to make patterns, such as stars, or spell out words. Avoid putting them in place until the icing is nearly dry, or they may sink in. If, on the other hand, the icing is completely dry, it may crack when placing the silver balls. Mimosa balls, resembling fluffy yellow mimosa flowers in size and appearance, come in other colours besides yellow. Piped sugar flowers also come in white and pastel shades, but do not always blend happily with your own piping. Non-edible decorations include flowers, miniature green and silver leaves, silver bells and horseshoes, and candle holders of all sizes and colours.

This chapter is an extract from Audrey Ellis's informative book, "Modern Cake Decorating", published by Pearson.

98

WEDDING
AND OTHER CAKES
FOR BIG
OCCASIONS

It is useful to have a complete recipe to refer to at every stage while making, covering, and icing an elaborate cake. Wherever possible this has been done. However, since the full instructions are inevitably repetitive, certain recipes in this section omit them, giving instead easy references to other recipes which are printed in full. You will find in this book a considerable choice of ways to cover a cake with almond paste and royal icing. Experiment, trying alternative methods; but always study the instructions very closely before beginning to carry out the decorations.

PERFECTION WEDDING CAKE
Colour plate twenty-two/three

See chart overleaf for quantities. Line 3 round tins, 6 in., 9 in., 12 in. Prepare the dried fruit. Cut cherries in half. Blanch and chop almonds. Sieve dry ingredients. Cream butter and sugar (sieve first if lumpy) then beat in eggs. Stir in milk or brandy. Add a little gravy browning, if liked, to give a darker colour. Fold in dry ingredients, then almonds and mixed fruit. Put mixture in prepared tins. Bake at Mark 1, 290 deg., for 1 hour. Reduce to Mark ½, 265 deg., for rest of time. Allow cake to cool in tin for 1 hour. When cold, remove greaseproof paper, pierce base with skewer and sprinkle with brandy. Wrap in greaseproof paper and foil and store in cool dry place. The cakes can be prepared one day and cooked on the following day if this is more convenient. Cover with greaseproof paper and store in cool place. If stored in refrigerator, remove and leave for 1 hour before baking.

Almond Paste: Sift the icing sugar, add the castor sugar and ground almonds and bind to a fairly stiff paste with beaten egg. Avoid handling too much otherwise the almond paste will 'oil'.

Royal Icing: Leave the egg whites to stand overnight. Add the glycerine and stir in about half the sifted icing sugar. Beat until smooth and glossy, then add enough of the sifted icing sugar to give a mixture that will hold peaks. The quantities given in the chart should be sufficient to give one coat of icing and simple decoration.

To ice: If necessary trim the tops of cakes to make them even. Use a little almond paste to build up the sides. On a sugared board, roll out about two-thirds of almond paste into a strip (do this in two parts for the large cake) the depth of the cake. Trim. Brush strip with warmed, sieved apricot jam and fit to the sides of cakes. Roll out rest of almond paste to fit top. Brush with apricot jam and invert cake on to it. Trim edges. Lift right way up and smooth well. Allow to dry.

Make up the royal icing. Spread evenly on top of the cake and smooth with the thin edge of large knife or clean ruler – take across in one sweep. Spread icing round sides and smooth with a palette knife, held upright, or with a plastic scraper. It is easier to ice sides of the cake if you have a turntable. Rotate turntable as you work. To decorate, mark the positions of the pillars on the 12 and 9 in. cakes. Pipe 4-pointed star in the

Wedding cake chart

	Round 6 in	Square 6 in / Round 7 in	Square 7 in / Round 8 in	Square 8 in / Round 9 in	Square 9 in / Round 10 in	Square 10 in / Round 11 in	Square 11 in / Round 12 in	Square 12 in
Mixed fruit cherries, peel	13 oz	1 lb 3 oz	1 lb 12 oz	2 lb 6 oz	3 lb 9 oz	4 lb 12 oz	5 lb	7 lb 2 oz
Almonds	1 oz	2 oz	3 oz	4 oz	6 oz	8 oz	10 oz	12 oz
Plain flour	4 oz	6 oz	9 oz	12 oz	1 lb 2 oz	1 lb 8 oz	1 lb 14 oz	2 lb 4 oz
Salt	pinch	pinch	pinch	pinch	¼	¼	½	1
					teaspoonful			
Spice	½	¾	1	1½	2	3	4	4½
				teaspoonful				
Butter	3 oz	4 oz	6 oz	8 oz	12 oz	1 lb	1 lb 4 oz	1½ lb
Soft brown sugar	3 oz	4 oz	6 oz	8 oz	12 oz	1 lb	1 lb 4 oz	1½ lb
Standard eggs	2	3	4	6	9	12	15	18
Milk or brandy	1	1½	2	3	4½	6	7½	9
				tablespoonful				
Gravy browning	few drops							
Baking times	3-3½ hr	3½-4 hr	4-4¼ hr	4¼-4½ hr	4½-5 hr	6-6½ hr	7-7½ hr	7½-8 hr
Appr. number of servings	25-30	35-40	40-50	60-70	70-80	100-110	110-120	140-150

Almond paste

Icing sugar	4 oz	5 oz	7 oz	8 oz	9 oz	11 oz	12 oz	14 oz
Castor sugar	4 oz	5 oz	7 oz	8 oz	9 oz	11 oz	12 oz	14 oz
Ground almonds	8 oz	10 oz	14 oz	1 lb	1 lb 2 oz	1 lb 6 oz	1 lb 8 oz	1 lb 12 oz
Eggs	1-2	1-2	2	2-3	2-3	3	3-4	4

Royal icing

Egg whites	1-2	1-2	2-3	3-4	4	5-6	6	7
Glycerine	1	1	1½	2	2¼	2¾	3	3½
				teaspoonful				
Icing sugar	1 lb	1 lb 4 oz	1 lb 12 oz	2 lb	2 lb 4 oz	2 lb 12 oz	3 lb	3 lb 8 oz

centre of these tiers. Lovers' knots: Pipe with No. 5 rope tube on the sides of each cake. Fine shell edge: Pipe with a No. 6 star tube to edge the boards and the trellis. Large shell edge: using a No. 12 shell tube, edge the top and base of each cake. Forget-me-nots: Pipe with a No. 2 writer tube in groups of 4 or 5 dots in pale blue on the sides of each cake. Leaves: Ice with a No. 17 leaf tube in pale green on the sides of each cake. Trellis: Fill in stars with trellis using a No. 2 writer tube. Place decoration in the centre of the top tier.

TWO-TIER BRIDE'S CAKE

You require: For cake: 1 lb. plain flour • 1 rounded teasp. mixed spice • 1 level teasp. cinnamon • 1 level dessp. cocoa powder • 12 oz. butter or margarine • 12 oz. soft brown sugar • 6 eggs • 1 tbsp. black treacle • ½ gill sherry or brandy • 1 teasp. almond essence • 2 oz. blanched and chopped almonds • 2 oz. ground almonds • 1 lb. sultanas • 12 oz. currants • 8 oz. seedless raisins • 2 oz. preserved and chopped ginger • 4 oz. glacé cherries, halved • 2 oz. chopped mixed peel • the finely grated rind of 1 orange • For almond paste: 1 lb ground almonds • ½ lb. castor sugar • ½ lb. sieved icing sugar • 2 eggs • 2 teasp. brandy • 1 teasp. vanilla essence • ½ teasp. almond essence • For royal icing: Approx. 2 lb. sieved icing sugar • 5 egg whites • few drops blue colouring (laundry blue is excellent) • 4 drops glycerine •

Wash and dry the currants, sultanas and raisins. Sieve together the flour, mixed spice, cinnamon and cocoa powder. Cream butter or margarine and sugar together till pale and fluffy, then add the eggs, one at a time, beating thoroughly after each addition to prevent curdling. Lightly fold in half the flour mixture, then stir in the black treacle, sherry or brandy, almond essence and chopped and ground almonds. Thoroughly mix in all the dried fruit, the ginger, cherries, mixed peel and orange rind. Stir in remaining flour, then turn the mixture into 2 round tins, 7 in. diameter and 9 in. diameter, well greased and lined with double greaseproof paper. Bake at Mark 4, 350 deg. for 30 minutes, then at Mark 2, 310 deg., for a further 2¼-3¼ hours, removing the smaller cake when ready, about 2¾ hours in all. Cool the cakes on wire trays, wrap in grease-

Two-tier Bride's Cake

proof paper and store in tins for at least a fort-
night.

Make almond paste: Mix together the almonds
and sugars thoroughly, then form into a fairly
stiff paste with the eggs, lightly beaten with the
brandy and essences. Knead firmly till smooth
and even. Brush top and sides of both cakes with
melted and sieved apricot jam, then very neatly
cover the larger cake with two-thirds of the almond paste, and the smaller cake with the remaining third of the paste. Place on boards, each
two inches larger all round than the cakes, and
set both aside for at least a week.

Make royal icing: Lightly beat the egg whites,
then add the icing sugar by spoonfuls, beating
thoroughly till a smooth, semi-stiff but pliable
icing is formed. Stir in sufficient blue colouring
to make the mixture very white, then add the
glycerine to prevent the icing from becoming
very hard and difficult to cut. Spread the icing
over the top and sides of the cakes, smoothing
with a palette knife, dipped from time to time
in hot water and shaken dry. Leave for a few
days for the icing to harden before piping.

To pipe, make up the icing as previously directed
using about ½–¾ of the quantity, but omitting
the glycerine and adding 2 teaspoons lemon
juice. Pipe top and sides of 2 cakes as liked with
rosettes, lines of trellis, dots, etc. Decorate with
silver leaves and slippers, then fix 3 small pillars
on the lower tier using icing to hold them in
place. When set and hard, place the smaller tier
on the pillars and top with a bridal decoration.

SWEETHEARTS' WEDDING CAKE
Colour plate twenty-four

You require: 6 in. and 11 in. square cakes made according to chart on page 100 • almond paste • 4 lb.
icing sugar • 8 egg whites • 2 teasp. glycerine • a few
teasp. lemon juice • 2 doz. pink heart plaques, 4 large,
12 medium, 8 small • 4 3 in. square pillars • 16 tiny
silver leaves • 16 larger leaves • 8 small horseshoes •
8 small pink sugar roses • 1 square 13 in. cake board •
1 square 7 in. cake board • pink ribbon decoration
for top cake •

Coat both cakes with almond paste and store for
several days before icing. Make a template of the
design for the tops of both cakes, marking the
centre of each side as a guide to position central
heart directly under it. Mark off a triangle at each
corner 4½ in. across the long side, using a No. 1
writing tube. Fill in with straight parallel lines
right to corners. On sides of larger cake, place
the heart plaques (1 large and 2 medium) in position on each side, with a dab of soft icing, and
using same writing tube, outline with tiny dots.
Outline the edge of the triangles on top of the
cake with the same dots. With a No. 6 star tube,
outline the top edge of the cake with a double
row of small stars and the bottom edge with 2
rows of shell piping, using the same star tube.
Mount pairs of small silver leaves at the top and
larger leaves at the bottom corners, centred with
a sugar rose. Arrange the 4 pillars evenly in place
to hold the top tier, and affix with a dab of icing.
Mount a horseshoe at the base of each pillar.
Repeat the decorations on top tier in the same
way, omitting the pillars and adding the required
central decoration and a horseshoe half-way along
the top edge of each side.

*Draw hearts of various sizes on stiff paper,
cover with larger sheets of waxed paper marked
off into squares. Trace outline of heart with
glacé icing and fine writing tube and at once
fill in with softer icing. Move waxed paper across
and repeat process until you have sufficient*

Posy Christening Cake

POSY CHRISTENING CAKE

You require: 8 oz. plain flour • 3 oz. fine semolina • 8 oz. butter or margarine • 8 oz. castor sugar • 4 standard eggs • 12 oz. each currants and sultanas, cleaned • 4 oz. mixed peel, chopped • 4 oz. glacé cherries, quartered • 2 oz. almonds, blanched and finely chopped • 1 tbsp. rose water • 2 lb. almond paste • 2¼ lb. royal icing •

Sift flour and semolina. Cream fat and sugar till light and fluffy. Beat in eggs, one at a time, sifting in one rounded tablespoon flour and semolina with each egg. Add fruit, peel, cherries, almonds and rose water and mix thoroughly. Lastly, stir in remaining flour and semolina. Transfer mixture to an 8 in. square tin, well greased and lined with a double thickness of greaseproof paper. Bake in the centre of the oven at Mark 2, 310 deg., for

2 hours, then at Mark 1, 290 deg., for a further hour. If the top of the cake appears to be browning too rapidly, cover with brown paper. Leave at least 15 minutes before turning out of the tin. Cool on a wire tray. Wrap in greaseproof paper or aluminium foil and store in an airtight tin for at least a week.

Cover neatly with almond paste, then put cake aside in a cool place for 4 days to a week until paste hardens.

Coat the cake with royal icing and then leave a few days for the icing to harden before decorating.

To decorate, stand cake on large square board, cover out to edges of board with thin coat of icing. Using a small star tube, pipe rosettes round top, corners and base of cake, and another line of rosettes under top edge. Decorate board with

spaced dots and border of dots, using No. 2 writer tube. Place posy of flowers on top of cake. It is a charming idea to make a number of miniature cakes as shown in the photograph to give as souvenirs to the God parents.

BLUE STORK CHRISTENING CAKE
Colour plate twenty-seven

You require: For cake: 10 oz. currants • 7 oz. sultanas • 4 oz. raisins • 2½ oz. glacé cherries • 2½ oz. whole almonds • 2½ oz. mixed cut peel • grated rind of 1 lemon • 2 tbsp. brandy • 7 oz. plain flour • 1 level teasp. mixed spice • 2 oz. ground almonds • 6 oz. luxury margarine • 6 oz. soft brown sugar • 1 tbsp. black treacle • 4 eggs • For covering 1¼-1½ lb. almond paste • For decoration: 1½ lb. royal icing • ¾ lb. satin icing, tinted pink •

Prepare the dried fruit; cut the cherries in four. Blanch the almonds, chop finely. Mix the prepared fruits, almonds, peel and lemon rind together in a mixing bowl and pour over the brandy. (If liked leave overnight.) Sieve the flour and spice and add the ground almonds. Place margarine and sugar in a bowl and cream together until light and fluffy. Beat in the treacle. Add the eggs, one at a time and beat in thoroughly, adding a little of the sieved flour with every egg after the first. Fold in the remaining flour mixture with the prepared fruit, etc., half at a time, gently and thoroughly until well mixed. Line the inside of the tin (8 in. round or 7 in. square tin) with double thickness of greaseproof paper and brush inside with melted margarine. Place the mixture evenly into prepared tin. Tie several thicknesses of thick paper or newspaper around the outside of the tin to prevent the cake from overbrowning. Smooth top of cake with the back of a wet spoon. Bake on the middle shelf of a very slow oven, Mark 1, 290 deg. Allow approximately 4 hours. Remove from oven. Leave in tin to cool slightly, turn out, take off paper, cool on a wire tray. When quite cold, wrap in double greaseproof paper and store in air-tight tin until required. Coat the cake with almond paste and royal icing in the usual way, giving 2 coats. Dry thoroughly. Make up some royal icing, position cake on a 10 in. board and cover board smoothly to edge with icing.

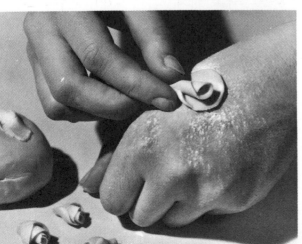

Reindeer Christmas Cake

Blue Stork Christening Cake

Disc Cake

Happy Birthday Book

Novelty Musical Gâteau

Make up about ¾ lb. satin icing tinted pink. Make up 23 roses, with a few extra to allow for breakages, as follows. To make the petals, place a piece of satin icing the size of a large mimosa ball on the back of the hand. Flatten out thinly to a smooth petal shape, with the forefinger of the other hand. Make 3 petals to form one rose. After making the first petal, roll it round and round to form the centre of the rose. Then fold the other petals round the first, turning the tips slightly outwards. Leave to dry and carefully cut off the stems, if too long.

Mark off top and base of cake into 8 even sections with small dots of icing. Using a No. 6 star tube, pipe a border round top outer edge of cake, following an inverted 'e' pattern going from small to large, to small again. Repeat this process 8 times around the cake until the border is covered, and the same pattern round the base of the cake. With a No. 1 writing tube, pipe 8 loops to the top border pattern. With the same tube, pipe small dots of icing over the piped loops. Position stork ornament with a dab of icing. Pipe dots of icing tinted pale blue round its base. Decorate top of cake with 5 groups of 3 roses, placed 1 in. in from the border, leaving space for child's name. Attach with dots of blue icing; using same tube, pipe in name. Position 8 roses round the base of the cake with dots of blue icing on either side. Fix narrow blue ribbon round sides of cake.

To make Christening cake for a girl, as shown right, tint the royal icing pink, reserving a small amount of white for decorating, and a further small amount tinted a darker pink. Place cake on board and cover out to edge with darker pink icing. With same icing, using No. 5 rope tube, pipe shells round top edge, using a shaking movement before drawing out icing to a point 1 in. long. Pipe round border base of cake with same tube, using inverted 'e' pattern. Using No. 2 writer tube, pipe name of child, with groups of dots and a scroll at centre front of cake, place stork ornament behind, and mask edge with dots. Using No. 3 writer tube, and white icing, over-pipe loops and dots round base of cake and shells round edge of the board. If liked, to make the child's name more prominent over-pipe with a fine writing tube, in a lighter colour.

Pink Stork Christening Cake

CHOCOLATE CHRISTENING CAKE

You require: For cake: 8 oz. butter or margarine • 8 oz. sugar • 4 eggs • 7 oz. self-raising flour • 2 oz. cocoa • 2 oz. ground almonds • 1 teasp. baking powder • For American frosting: 1½ lb. lump sugar • ¼ pint water • 3 egg whites • For decoration: stork ornament • pink or blue sugar flowers • paper doiley •

Pink Rose Birthday Cake

Cream the fat and sugar until light and fluffy. Beat in the lightly beaten eggs a little at a time. Fold in the sieved flour, cocoa, baking powder and ground almonds, and add sufficient warm water to form a soft dropping consistency. Turn into three greased 8 in. sandwich tins, and bake at Mark 5, 375 deg., for 20-25 minutes. Cool on a wire tray.

Make the frosting. Place the sugar in a saucepan and add the water. Heat gently until the sugar dissolves, and then boil until a little of the mixture forms a soft ball when dropped into cold water. Allow to cool, but not to thicken. Whisk the egg whites until stiff. Gradually add the syrup, whisking all the time until the mixture stands up in peaks. Spread evenly between the sandwich layers, and stand the cake on a silver cake board. Spread the remaining frosting over the top and around the sides of the cake, and pull into peaks with the back of a teaspoon. Make whirls of the icing pulled up to a central peak evenly spaced round the sides and top of the cake. Place sugar roses in alternate whirls round sides, and in every whirl on

top of cake. Trim edge with paper doiley and place stork ornament on top.

PINK ROSE BIRTHDAY CAKE
(See jacket illustration)

You require: 8 oz. butter or margarine • 8 oz. soft brown sugar • 4 eggs • 8 oz. plain flour • 1 dessp. cocoa • ½ teasp. ground mace • ½ teasp. ground mixed spice • 1 teasp. coffee essence • 8 oz. raisins • 8 oz. sultanas • 1 lb. currants • ¼ lb. mixed peel • ¼ lb. glacé cherries • 2 oz. whole almonds • rind and juice of half a lemon • 1½ lb. almond paste • 1 lb. flat icing • 1 lb. royal icing • few drops pink vegetable colouring • 8 large sugar roses • candles and candle holders as required •

Cream the fat and brown sugar until light and fluffy. Beat in the eggs one at a time. Fold in the sieved flour, spice, cocoa and coffee. Add the lemon rind and juice. Stir in the cleaned dried fruit, glacé cherries, peel and then the blanched split almonds. Turn into a double lined 8 in. cake tin. Fold a sheet of brown paper into several thicknesses and tie round the outside of the tin. Stand on a wad of newspaper and bake in a very mod-

106

erate oven, Mark 3, 335 deg. for 1 hour and reduce to very cool, Mark ½, 265 deg., and continue to bake for a further 4 hours. Allow to cool before removing from tin. Store in an airtight tin until required. Cover with almond paste in the usual way, taking care to make quite smooth and level. Dry out, then coat with the flat icing, tinted pale pink. Tint the royal icing the same colour. Place cake on a board only a little larger. Using turntable, pipe sides with diamond trellis, with a No. 1 writer tube. Edge top and base with shells, using No. 5 rope tube. Position the roses with dabs of icing evenly spaced out round the sides of the cake, taking care not to crack the trellis. Mask the edge of the board with another row of smaller shells, again using rope tube. Pipe child's name in centre of cake, using No. 1 writer tube, space candle holders evenly round top 1 in. in from the edge.

COFFEE ENGAGEMENT CAKE
Colour plate nineteen

You require: For filling: 6 oz. coffee butter cream • To cover cake: 12 oz. white glacé icing • For decorations: 4 oz. coffee glacé icing •

Make up coffee-flavoured Victoria sponge mixture (see page 13) in an 8 in. deep round tin. Cut the cake in half and spread with butter cream. Sandwich together again. Make up the white glacé icing, pour on to the top of the cake and spread very carefully over top and sides, to coat smoothly. Place cake on a wire tray over a plate to catch icing drips. Make up the coffee glacé icing to a stiff consistency.
Using paper template divide top edge of cake into 8 sections, and mark out 8 points equidistant between the sections on a concentric circle of 2½ in. radius. Using the coffee glacé icing and a No. 8 star tube, pipe round edge of top of cake, making 7 large rosettes in each section. Fill in a second row of rosettes, centred on each basic row of 7 then 2 rosettes and finally 1 rosette at the point marked on the inner circle. Repeat in each section to form a central star pattern. Trim round bottom edge of cake neatly, transfer to a turntable raised on a book if necessary so that sides can be iced at a comfortable height when seated. With a No. 3 writer tube, pipe in the names of the couple or other appropriate message. Make a side template, write the word CONGRATULATIONS spaced out to fill half length, prick out round the sides of the cake. To make sure the letters are evenly spaced divide half the circumference of the cake into 15 equal parts, one for each letter. Ice the word in with the same writing tube.

TWENTY-FIRST BIRTHDAY CAKE
Colour plate twenty-one

You require: For decoration: 3 lb. almond paste • 3 lb. royal icing • colouring • sugar roses • wide pink ribbon •

Make up a 10 in. square fruit cake according to the three-tier wedding cake chart. Coat the cake with almond paste and store for a few days.
Position the cake on a 12 in. board with icing, spread top and sides smoothly, take icing out to the edges of the board. Allow to harden. Stiffen up the icing to a firm piping consistency and, using a Number 12 star tube, pipe a border of large rosettes round top and bottom edges of the cake. To finish the top edge, pipe smaller rosettes, using a number 6 star tube, opposite the large ones, but 1½ in. in from the edge. Pipe a similar band of small rosettes round the sides of the cake 1½ in. below the top edge. Leave to dry. Thin down the icing a little and with a number 1 writer tube pipe diagonal strands of icing from the large to the small stars in one direction, all round the cake. Leave to dry, then pipe diagonal strands in the opposite direction. Sketch out the lettering HAPPY BIRTHDAY on a sheet of white paper and cover with waxed paper, placing both sheets on a baking tin so that paper is kept flat. Using a number 3 writer tube and icing tinted apricot pink, pipe on to the waxed paper, tracing out greeting on white paper underneath. Leave 48 hours to dry out, then fix in position with icing, from corner to corner. The 21 is similarly piped out in outline on to waxed paper with a number 1 writer tube and the centre flooded with softer icing. Harden off and place in lower front corner. (Use same icing and number 1 writer tube to fill edges of board with maze pattern.) Decorate remaining corner with group of large sugar-paste roses tinted to

match pink icing, and leaves tinted green. Fix a wide pink ribbon round the cake.

STARTIME CHRISTMAS CAKE
Colour plate twenty-eight/nine

You require: For cake: 8 oz. butter or margarine • 8 oz. soft brown sugar • 4 eggs • 8 oz. plain flour • 1 dessp. cocoa • ½ teasp ground mace • 1 teasp. coffee essence or extract • ½ teasp. ground mixed spice • 8 oz. raisins • 8 oz. sultanas • 1 lb. currants • ¼ lb. mixed peel • ¼ lb. glacé cherries • 2 oz. whole almonds • rind and juice of ½ lemon • jam • For covering: 1½ lb. almond paste • For flat icing: 1 lb. icing sugar • 2 egg whites • For royal icing: 1½ lb. icing sugar • 3 egg whites • For decorations: holly sprigs • red ribbon • candle in holder •

Cream the fat and sugar until light and fluffy. Beat in the eggs one at a time. Fold in the sieved flour, spice, cocoa and coffee. Add the lemon rind and juice. Stir in the cleaned, dried fruit, glacé cherries, candied peel and split almonds. Turn into a double lined 8 in. cake tin. Fold a sheet of brown paper into several thicknesses and tie around the outside of the tin. Stand on a wad of newspaper and bake in oven at Mark 3, 335 deg., for one hour, reduce to very cool and continue to bake for a further four hours. Allow to cool before removing from the tin. Store in airtight tin until required.

To cover, spread the cake with a thin layer of jam and coat with the almond paste in the usual way. Allow three days to elapse before icing.

To ice with flat icing, stand the cake on its upturned tin. Put the icing sugar into the bowl and

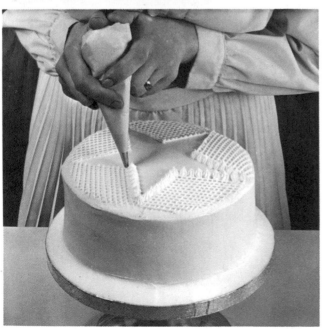

add sufficient egg white to form a stiff consistency. Beat throughly. Pile on to the centre of the cake. Using a palette knife, spread evenly over the top and remove excess from the sides. Draw a hot wet ruler across the surface to ensure a flat top. Remove any surplus from the edges. Spread the remaining icing around the sides and smooth with a palette knife. Trim the bottom edge.

To decorate, make up royal icing in the same way as for flat icing. Stand the cake on a board at least 2 in. larger than the cake. Spread icing round the edge of the board to give a decorative finish. Cut out a pattern for the star from thin cardboard, about 5 in. across. Place on top of the cake and prick around the edge with a pin. Remove star shape. Using a No. 2 writer tube, pipe over the pricks to show clearly the star outline. Use the same tube to pipe straight lines across the rest of the cake until the whole of the area outside the star is covered. Then pipe at right angles to form trellis pattern. Using No. 8 star tube, pipe stars around the edge of the star shape. Top every other one with a silver ball. Using No. 21 star piping tube, pipe shell edging around top and bottom edges. Complete the decoration with holly leaves, red ribbon and a candle in fancy holder.

YULE LOG
Colour plate twenty-eight / nine

You require: For log: 3 eggs • 3 oz. castor sugar • vanilla essence • 2½ oz. plain flour • 1 tbsp. cocoa • 1 tbsp. warm water • For filling and icing: 4 oz. butter • 8 oz. icing sugar • 1 tbsp. cocoa •

Grease and line a Swiss roll tin approx. 12 in. × 9 in. Whisk the eggs, sugar and vanilla essence until thick, light and fluffy. Fold in the sieved flour and cocoa. Carefully stir in the warm water. Pour into the prepared tin. Bake in oven at Mark 6, 400 deg., for about 10 minutes. When cooked, turn at once on to a piece of sugared greaseproof paper. Trim the edges of the sponge with a sharp knife and carefully roll up so that the paper is rolled inside.

While the sponge is cooling, make up the butter cream by beating together the butter and icing sugar and adding a little milk or water if necessary to form a soft, dropping consistency. Divide this mixture. Blend the cocoa with a little boiling water. Mix well and allow to cool. Then beat the blended cocoa into one half of the butter cream, making chocolate cream. When the sponge is quite cool, gently unroll and spread with the white butter cream. Re-roll and spread the chocolate cream over the outside. Draw a fork along the surface to give the effect of bark on a log. Dust with sieved icing sugar to represent snow. Add a sprig of holly.

A home-made cake to decorate. In case you decide at the last minute to decorate your own Christmas cake, here is one that matures extra quickly.

LAST-MINUTE CAKE

You require: 1 lb. mixed dried fruit (currants, sultanas, seedless raisins) • 4 oz. glacé cherries • 2 oz. walnuts or almonds • 2 oz. candied peel • 8 oz. plain flour • 1 teasp. baking powder • good pinch salt • 1 teasp. mixed spice • 6 oz. soft brown sugar • 5 oz. vegetable fat • grated rind of 1 orange • 2 tbsp. orange juice • 3 eggs •

Grease and line an 8 in. round or 7 in. square cake tin. Prepare fruit. Halve cherries. Chop nuts and mix all together with the peel. Sift the flour, the baking powder, the salt and the spice together. Sift the sugar to remove any lumps. To flour mixture and sugar, add all remaining ingredients including a few drops of gravy browning if liked, but not the prepared fruit and nuts. Stir briskly for 1–2 minutes until smooth and creamy. Stir in fruit and nuts, put in prepared tin. Hollow centre. Bake at Mark 2, 310 deg., for 2¾–3 hours.

THREE WAYS TO FINISH
A CHRISTMAS CAKE

Although the two cakes shown in colour plate twenty-six look very different, they are in fact made from the same basic cake mixture. One is a ring cake with a piped design and the other requires no piping at all. Another variation is the Holly Wreath Christmas Cake shown on page 113.

BASIC TRADITIONAL CAKE

You require: 1 lb. dried fruit (currants, sultanas, seedless raisins) • 2 oranges • 4 oz. almonds and walnuts, mixed • 4 oz. glacé cherries • 1-2 oz. candied peel • 9 oz. plain flour • pinch salt • 1-1½ teasp. mixed spice • 6 oz. butter • 6 oz. sugar • 4 eggs • few drops gravy browning, optional •

Grease and line an 8 in. round or 7 in. square cake tin. Prepare dried fruit. Finely grate orange rind and add to fruit with juice. Mix well and leave to stand overnight. Blanch almonds and chop roughly with walnuts. Halve cherries and mix, with nuts and peel, into prepared fruit. Sift flour, salt and spice. Cream the butter and sugar. Beat in eggs. Fold in flour mixture. Add a few drops of gravy browning, if liked, to darken. Finally fold in the prepared fruit mixture and nuts. Put mixture into tin. Hollow the centre well with the back of a wooden spoon if using round tin. Bake at Mark 1, 290 deg., for 1 hour, then reduce heat to Mark ½, 265 deg., for a further 2¾-3¼ hours.

SNOW PEAK CHRISTMAS CAKE
Colour plate twenty-six

You require: 1½ lb. almond paste • sieved apricot jam • 1½ lb. royal icing •

Brush crumbs from the 8 in. round cake and coat with jam. Cover with almond paste in the usual

way, making sure that the covering is smooth and level. Coat with royal icing when the almond paste has sufficiently dried out. Using a thin skewer, swirl the icing first into rough peaks all over the cake, and then into circular whirls evenly spaced out round the sides and top of the cake.

GOLDEN BAUBLE CHRISTMAS CAKE
Colour plate twenty-six

You require: 1¾ lb. almond paste • sieved apricot jam • 2 lb. royal icing • 1½ doz. golden glass baubles•

Roll the almond paste out on a sugared board. Make greaseproof paper patterns of the top, sides, and inner circle of ring cake to be lined. Cut from the paste the shape required for the top, then cut a strip exactly to fit round the sides, or two pieces each half the circumference of the cake if this makes it easier to handle. Cut another strip to line centre. Brush centre hollow with sieved jam, press in lining.

Brush top of cake with sieved jam, press top covering of paste on cake. Brush sides of cake with sieved jam. Hold the cake on its sides, then, just as if rolling a hoop, roll the cake along the strip (or two strips) of paste. If you do this firmly, you will find the paste sticks evenly to the sides of the cake. Neaten sides by rolling jam jar, or rolling pin held upright, round the sides of the cake. Roll the top to give a neat finish. Allow the almond paste to harden, before decorating.

If you are confident you have handled the paste so lightly that it has not become sticky, you can coat with royal icing at once. The immediate icing method has the advantage of keeping the almond paste moist, but if it has been much handled, the oil will seep through and spoil the colour of the icing. Therefore if you are in any doubt it is wise to allow the paste up to four days to dry out. As a safeguard you can coat the paste with a seal of egg white, and let this dry slightly before putting on the icing.

Use approximately 1¼ lb. royal icing to coat the cake in the usual way, and allow to harden. Either keep remainder of icing soft by putting it in a basin and covering the top with a damp cloth, or make up the remaining ¾ lb. only when required.

Make a paper template for the top of the cake. Draw 4 wedge-shaped sections to be filled with diamond trellis, and fill in the spaces between the sections with several thick lines radiating from the centre, surrounded by dots. Prick out the design. Practise the trellis pattern as shown below

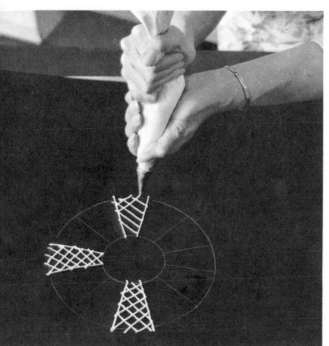

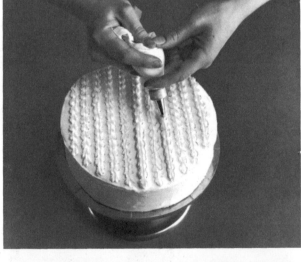

to gain confidence first, then pipe on the cake with No. 2 writer tube. With same tube pipe sides of cake with diamond trellis. Finish inner ring and edge base of cake with stars, using No. 8 star tube. Position baubles before icing dries.

HOLLY WREATH CHRISTMAS CAKE

You require: 1½ lb. almond paste • sieved apricot jam • 1¾ lb. royal icing • 16 marzipan holly leaves • 16 marzipan holly berries • wide red ribbon •

Brush crumbs from the 8 in. round cake and coat with jam. Cover with almond paste in the usual way, making sure that the covering is smooth and level. Tint a small portion of almond paste with holly red vegetable colouring, and a slightly larger amount with sap green vegetable colouring. Form tiny balls from the red almond paste for berries. Roll out the green almond paste, cut oval leaf shapes from it about 1 in. long, and with

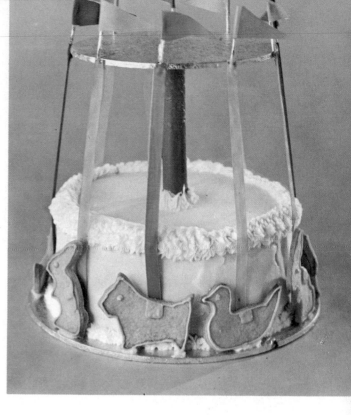

Merry-go-round

Igloo Cake

Chequer-board Cake

Humpty-Dumpty

Rocket Cake

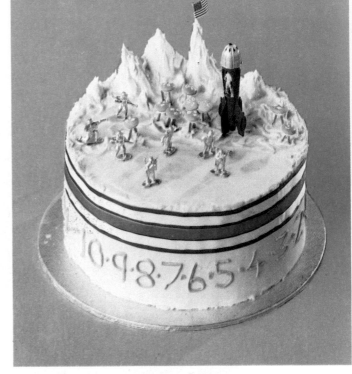

Clown Cake

Finished Holly Wreath Cake

the bowl of a small teaspoon, cut out shapes to give the spiky effect of holly leaves. Mark in with tip of a knife to represent veins, and curl leaves over slightly before leaving them to harden. Coat the cake with royal icing in the usual way, reserving ¾ lb. icing for the piping. The work can all be done with the same tube, a fairly large and bold one, such as No. 8 star tube.

Mark parallel lines 1 in. apart all over the top of the cake. Start with the centre line and work outwards towards either side to avoid damaging the work already done, using shell edging. Pipe two rows of shell edging round the top edge – one on the top of the cake and one on the side. Pipe a third row of shell edging round the base of the cake. Leave to set before removing from the turntable on to a serving dish. Take care not to crack the border edging of the base. Position the holly leaves and berries round the top of the

cake, evenly spaced out, just inside the edging, and put in place with dabs of icing. Alternatively, press in place just before the top shell edging is quite dry. Cut a length of wide red ribbon 1 in. longer than circumference of cake, fix one end with a dab of icing against side of cake, allow to dry. Draw ribbon taut round cake, turn in raw end and fix over neatly with Sellotape.

How to pipe rosettes and shells

Always work from left to right, or towards you, holding the icing bag or syringe at a steep angle. To make rosettes or stars, hold the bag vertically on top, or horizontally if working against the side of the cake. Place tube close to surface of cake, press and pull away quickly to make a small rosette, well pointed in the centre. To make a larger one, press out more icing before pulling tube away. Shells are made by beginning as for a rosette, carrying the tube a fraction back and away from you and bringing over and towards you again, releasing the pressure and drawing away the tube. Make sure that each shell is piped to cover the tail of the last one, to give an even effect.

CHRISTMAS CAROL CAKE

You require: For cake: 10 oz. plain flour • 2 oz. fine semolina • 2 level teasp. mixed spice • pinch salt • ½ lb. butter • ½ lb. brown sugar • 5 medium eggs • 2 level tbsp. golden syrup or orange marmalade • 1 lb. currants, washed and dried • ½ lb. each, sultanas and raisins, washed and dried • ¼ lb. dessert prunes, stoned and chopped • ½ lb. dates, chopped • ¼ lb. glacé cherries, sliced • ¼ lb. mixed peel • 2 oz. chopped walnuts • grated rind of 1 orange and 1 lemon • For almond paste: 3 oz. fine semolina • 9 oz. ground almonds • 1½ lb. icing sugar, sieved • 1 egg beaten with 1 yolk • 3 dessp. lemon juice • few drops vanilla and almond essences • For Royal icing: 1½ lb. icing sugar, sieved • 4 egg whites • ¼ teasp. glycerine • For decoration: 5 angel ornaments • model Christmas tree • chocolate butter cream •

Christmas Carol Cake

Sift dry ingredients together. Cream fat and sugar together till light and fluffy then beat in eggs, one at a time, adding a tablespoon of flour mixture with each. Stir in syrup or marmalade. Add half the flour mixture then all the fruit, peel, nuts and grated orange and lemon rinds. Lastly, stir in rest of flour mixture. Turn into a 9 in. round cake tin, well greased and lined with at least a double thickness of greaseproof paper. Bake in the centre of the oven at Mark 2, 310 deg., for 2½ hours, then Mark 1, 390 deg., for a further 2½ hours. If cake browns too quickly on the top, cover with greaseproof or brown paper. Leave to cool slightly in the tin before turning out. Make almond paste: Mix together semolina, almonds and sugar. Form into a paste with remaining ingredients, then knead till smooth and pliable. Brush cake with heated and sieved jam or golden syrup then cover top and sides with the paste. Wrap cake in greaseproof paper and leave at least 3 days for the surface to dry.

Make royal icing: Lightly whisk egg whites then gradually stir in icing sugar. Beat well till the icing is smooth and white, then add the glycerine. Stand cake on a board, then spread top and sides with icing. Run a serrated icing ruler round sides to give ridged effect, then using a knife form a swirly border round top edge. Stand a group of angel ornaments or figures of your own choice, round a Christmas tree then, using chocolate butter cream in an icing syringe or bag with a writer tube, pipe notes of music round sides.

Tested tip

Straight lines formed with writing tubes are difficult to pipe neatly because of the long, continuous movement. Hold tube at same angle as a pen, let it touch the cake at the commencement of the movement only, then lift tube away, exerting pressure, drop point of tube back on to cake to break thread quickly. Do not let thread touch the surface of cake in the middle of any movement or the shape will be spoilt.

NOVELTY
CAKES

Every novelty cake should possess a theme, and tell its own story. It can be elaborate, but some of the best ideas are quite simple, and can be adapted to almost any festive occasion. A perfect example is the cake shown above, which is equally suitable for Christmas or a birthday.

When fastening inedible decorations to the sides of a cake, such as a ribbon bow or glass bauble, it is often easier to use a long pin. However, it is safer to affix ornaments with dabs of icing or if you use pins remember to be very careful to remove them before the cake is eaten. Also, keep an eye on children who may try to eat eskimos, tiny Christmas trees, or even candles, imagining that they must taste just as nice as the rest of the cake!

BELLS AND BOWS CAKE

You require: For cake: ½ lb. butter or margarine • ½ lb. brown sugar • 1 teasp. vanilla essence • 1 teasp. almond essence • 2 tbsp. orange marmalade • 4 eggs • 8 oz. plain flour • 2 oz. fine semolina • 4 level teasp. mixed spice • ¼ level teasp. salt • 1 level teasp. bicar-bonate soda • ½ lb. each raisins, sultanas, currants and dates • ¼ lb. each cherries, glacé mixed peel, ginger • ¼ lb. chopped almonds • 4 tbsp. brandy, sherry, or strong black coffee • For almond paste: 3 oz. fine semolina • 9 oz. ground almonds • 1½ lb. icing sugar, crushed and sifted • 1 egg beaten with 1 yolk • 3 dessp. lemon juice • few drops vanilla and almond essences • For royal icing: 3 egg whites • 1½ lb. icing sugar, crushed and sifted • 3 drops of glycerine • For decoration: silver bells • red and green bows made from ribbon • spray of holly or mistletoe •

Prepare cake tin with 3 linings of paper at bottom and sides. Beat butter and sugar and essences to a smooth cream. Beat in the marmalade. Beat in the eggs one at a time. Stir in the sifted flour, semolina, spice, salt and crushed bicarbonate of soda. Add the prepared fruit (seeded and chopped), peel and almonds. Stir in liquid. Turn into prepared 8 in. round tin, smoothing down evenly. Bake at Mark 2, 310 deg., in the centre of the oven, covering for the first half of cooking time with 2 thicknesses of paper. Baking time, 4 hours.

Blue Band Bunny Cake

Make royal icing: Lightly whisk the egg wites and gradually add the crushed and siftedreving sugar. Stir in a few drops of glycerine to pohient the icing becoming too hard. Beat thoroughly and use at once. Swirl the icing over the cake, using a round-topped knife. Decorate with silver bells and red and green bows of ribbon. Top with holly or mistletoe.

BLUE BAND BUNNY CAKE

You require: For 'One-Stage' Cake: 6 oz. luxury margarine • 6 oz. castor sugar • 3 large eggs • 6 oz. self-raising flour • 1½ teasp. baking powder • For 'One-Stage' Icing: 4 oz. luxury margarine • 8 oz. sieved icing sugar • 3 dessp. milk • pink vegetable colouring • For decoration: 6 oz. desiccated coconut • pink vegetable colouring • coloured sweets • 2 pieces long spaghetti, tinted green • ears cut from white cardboard •

Make the cake: place all the ingredients together in a mixing bowl, having first sieved the flour and baking powder together. Beat with a wooden spoon until well mixed (2-3 minutes). Grease a ½ pint and a 1½ pint pudding basin with melted luxury margarine. Divide the mixture proportionately between the two basins. Place basins on a baking tray. Bake on the middle shelf of a preheated very moderate oven, Mark 3, 335 deg., for about 35-40 minutes for the small cake and 1-1¼ hours for the large cake. Cool on a wire tray.

Make the icing: place all the ingredients in a mixing bowl and beat together with a wooden spoon until smooth. Tint most of the icing and coconut pink, reserving a little of each for the face and front of the bunny, the natural colour. Trim the cakes to form the body and head of the bunny. Cover the cakes and the cardboard ears all over with the icing and roll or press on the coconut. Use pink for the body and ears, white for face and front as shown in the photograph. Place the finished cake on a cake board or plate with a little icing. Press ears into position, cover joins with more coconut. Stick on the coloured sweets to represent eyes, nose and buttons, and pieces of spaghetti broken into suitable lengths for whiskers.

If you put the bunny on a board, cover the edge

The cake is cooked when firm and elastic to touch and has shrunken slightly from the sides of the tin and when a bright skewer pierced into the centre comes out undimmed.

Note. It is essential that the heat of the oven does not build up and overcook the cake. If you find it difficult to keep the temperature very low, stand the cake on a board or on extra thicknesses of paper on an oven tray during the last half of cooking.

Make almond paste: Mix together semolina, almonds and sugar. Form into a paste with remaining ingredients, then knead till smooth and pliable. Brush cake with heated and sieved jam or golden syrup then cover top and sides with paste. Wrap cake in greaseproof paper and leave at least 3 days to dry.

with silver paper edging, and the board itself with more coconut. It makes an effective finish to the cake if you arrange some tiny chocolate eggs in brightly coloured wrappings, nearby.

VALENTINE TRUE LOVE CAKE

You require: For cake: 4 oz. butter or margarine • 4 oz. castor sugar • 2 eggs • 5 oz. self-raising flour • 1 oz. cocoa • warm water • For filling and decoration: 4 oz. almond paste • cochineal • plain and chocolate butter cream • sugar flowers •

Cream together the butter and sugar until light and fluffy. Gradually beat in the lightly whisked eggs. Fold in the sieved flour and cocoa, and add sufficient warm water to give a soft dropping consistency. Turn into two lined and greased 7 in. sandwich tins, and bake at Mark 5, 375 deg., for 25-30 minutes. Turn on to a wire tray and allow to cool.

Knead a little cochineal into half the almond paste to give a pink colour. Roll out the pink and white almond paste and cut into heart shapes, making two larger ones for the top of the cake. Allow to dry before use. Fill the cake with butter cream and spread chocolate butter cream on the top. Arrange the small pink and white hearts alternately around the edge and the two larger ones in the centre. Complete the decoration by piping in an arrow with darker chocolate butter cream and adding a spray or two of sugar flowers.

VALENTINE HEART CAKE

You require: For cake: 2 eggs • their weight, in shells, in super sifted self-raising flour, butter or margarine • castor sugar • 3 or 4 drops of vanilla essence or grated rind of ½ lemon • pinch salt • For almond paste: 1 oz. ground almonds • 1 oz. castor sugar • 3 level teasp. condensed milk • red colouring • For royal icing: 6 oz. sieved icing sugar • 1 egg white • drop of lemon juice • Decoration: sugar flowers • angelica •

Sieve flour and salt, beat fat until soft, add sugar and beat again until light in colour and fluffy in texture. Add eggs one at a time together with a tablespoon of sieved flour, etc. Stir, add essence, beat thoroughly. Stir in remainder of flour. Put the mixture into the tin and smooth level. Bake at Mark 5, 375 deg., for 30 minutes.

Make almond paste: Mix ground almonds and sugar and bind with the condensed milk and colouring. Roll out and cut out a heart measuring 2½ in. × 3 in. using a sandwich cutter or cardboard guide. From the trimmings cut smaller hearts.

Make royal icing: Break up the egg white with a fork and gradually add the sugar. Add the lemon juice and beat the icing thoroughly until it is thick and white, and holds the mark of the spoon. Place the cake on a 10 in. cake board making it adhere with a little icing. Cover cake with the icing. Smooth the centre and make swirls round the sides. Make an arrow from the angelica and press into the heart. Place in the centre of the

Valentine True Love Cake

Valentine Heart Cake

117

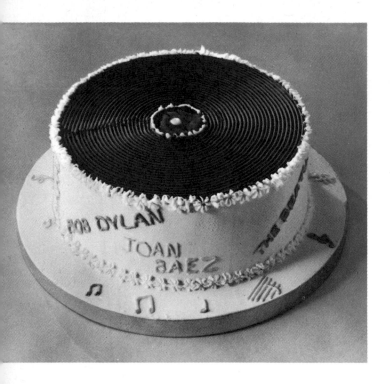

Disc Cake

Happy Birthday Book

cake and arrange flowers and small hearts round the sides.

Note: Bought almond paste may be used, colouring it with cochineal or red colouring. Heart-shaped sweets may also be used. It is therefore a very quick and easy cake to decorate.

NOVELTY MUSICAL GATEAU
Colour plate thirty

You require: For cake: 3 eggs • 3 oz. castor sugar • 3 oz. plain flour • 1 tbsp. cocoa • For butter cream: 2 oz. butter • 4 oz. icing sugar • a little milk • vanilla essence • For glacé icing and decoration: 4 oz. icing sugar • 1 teasp. cocoa • pkt. of chocolate finger biscuits •

Whisk the eggs and sugar until thick and creamy. Fold in the sieved flour and cocoa. Turn mixture into two greased 7 in. sandwich tins and bake at Mark 6, 400 deg., for about 10-12 minutes. Allow to cool.

To make the butter cream, soften the butter and beat in the sieved icing sugar. Add a little milk and vanilla essence to give a soft dropping consistency. Sandwich cakes together with butter cream and spread more butter cream round the outside edge. Stick finger biscuits round the cake.

To make the glacé icing, mix the sieved icing sugar with warm water to form a stiff consistency. Keep aside a tablespoon of icing and pour rest into centre of cake. Spread icing to outer edge of cake. Dissolve cocoa with a little boiling water and add to glacé icing, adding more icing sugar if necessary to make a stiff consistency. Put into greaseproof icing bag and cut a small hole in the end. When icing is set, pipe 'music' on to cake using the chocolate icing. Decorate with suitable small wooden figures.

Nine novelty designs for children

A dash of imagination – that's the magic ingredient needed to turn an everyday fruit or sponge cake into a delight for children. Bake or buy a cake in any of the usual shapes, then follow the simple directions here and on the following pages to create one of the delightful novelties illustrated for a child's birthday party, or any other festive occasion. Boys enjoy them as much as girls, and

Novelty Musical Gâteau

some of the designs will particularly appeal to boys, such as the Rocket Cake. The small toys you need to decorate some of the cakes are all quite inexpensive and easily obtained from a toy shop if the child does not already possess them.

HAPPY BIRTHDAY BOOK
Colour plate thirty

Use a rectangular cake. Coat sides with almond paste, shaping it outwards at bottom. Mark almond paste with a fork to represent leaves of the book. Paint with edible yellow food colouring. Place on slightly larger cake board. Place two strips of almond paste about 1 in. wide and ¼-½ in. thick on top of cake. Cover top of cake with rectangle of almond paste, curved over the strips to give the effect of an open book. Colour a little almond paste red, cut strips to fit round edges of cake board to make the cover of the book. Cut another strip of red almond paste for

ruler with the end just short of the centre, and the book mark. With number 2 writer tube and white royal icing, pipe round edge of cover and book mark in line-and-dot pattern. Pipe the birthday child's name down the book mark. Using number 3 writer tube and coloured royal icing, pipe appropriate dates and birthday wishes on the pages of book. Pipe daisy flower shapes, with sweets as centres, on pages of book, thickly overpiping several times to make bolder.

DISC CAKE
Colour plate thirty

Use a round cake. Coat with almond paste and royal icing. Pipe names of pop stars and groups round the sides of the cake and musical notes, etc., on the cake board in coloured royal icing using a number 2 writer tube. Coat top of cake with chocolate coloured royal icing and mark with lines to represent a disc. Place a serrated cake

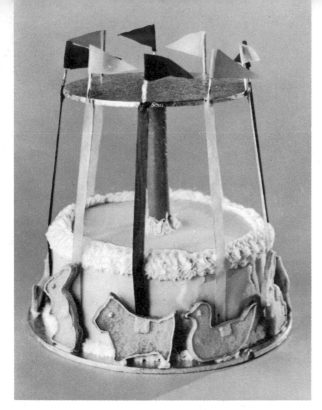

Merry-go-round

Igloo

Pipe round 'pole' where it enters icing and round top and bottom edges of cake, using a medium star or rose tube. Leave to set. Make 'animals' from either sweet shortcrust paste or biscuit mixture. Cut out with animal cutters. When they are cooked, pipe round edges of 'animals' with coloured royal icing using a No. 2 writer tube. Make top of Merry-go-round from a thin silver cake board, about 1 inch smaller than cake. Pin flags and ribbons in position. Secure cake board in position with icing. When set secure ribbons and 'animals' in place all round sides of cake with icing as in picture.

IGLOO CAKE
Colour plate thirty-one

Use a round cake. Coat with almond paste, moulding a thicker layer on top of cake to give a domed effect. Coat with royal icing. On one side of cake cut out a door through icing and almond paste. Using pale coffee-coloured royal icing and No. 1 or No. 2 writer tube, pipe lines over the igloo to make 'bricks'. Place cake on board, iced roughly with white royal icing. Put Eskimo figures and animals in position as in picture.

CHEQUER-BOARD CAKE
Colour plate thirty-one

Use a square cake. Coat with almond paste and royal icing. Using number 3 writing tube, pipe

ruler with the end just short of the centre, and hold it steady with your right hand while turning the table with the left hand, lifting it from the icing when the grooves meet. Fill in the centre with a little smooth icing. Pipe top and bottom edges of cake with rosettes of white royal icing. Using writer tube, pipe centre of cake as shown, to represent the centre of the disc.

MERRY-GO-ROUND
Colour plate thirty-one

Use a round cake. Coat with almond paste and royal icing. Before royal icing has set insert stick of red or striped rock through icing and cake.

Chequer-board Cake

straight lines across the top of cake in both directions to make the squares of the chequer-board, and when dry over-pipe with number 1 writing tube. Leave to set, while using a medium sized star tube to outline the top and bottom edges, the corners, and the sides close to the top, with stars. Now flood the alternate squares with soft chocolate-flavoured royal icing, as shown in the photograph. Leave again to set and harden. Place plain peppermint creams in one half of 'chequer-board' and chocolate peppermint creams in the other half, to represent draughts.

CLOWN CAKE
Colour plate thirty-two

Use a round cake. Coat with almond paste and royal icing. Round sides of cake, mark six circles and outline with coloured royal icing for the 'bodies'. When set, fill in the 'bodies' with softened royal icing in a different colour. Pipe a row of coloured dots down centre with royal icing.
Decorate top and bottom edges of cake using a medium rose or star tube. Paint faces on to table-tennis balls and place round top of cake, securing with little royal icing. Make conical hats from coloured paper or Cellophane and place on clowns' heads. If liked, place striped candle in centre of cake.

Clown Cake

HUMPTY-DUMPTY
Colour plate thirty-two

Use a round or square cake. Coat with almond paste and, if wished, mould a thicker layer of almond paste on the top of the cake to give a domed effect. Coat with royal icing. Using pale coffee-coloured royal icing and No. 1 or No. 2 writing nozzle, ice lines over the 'wall' to represent bricks. Place cake on board. Top with a Humpty-Dumpty made from a 'blown' egg shell which, if liked, can be painted white. Cut out 'eyes', 'nose' and 'mouth' from coloured paper and stick on to the egg shell, holding with a little royal icing. Top with 'hair' made from a fringed strip of yellow Cellophane. Make the 'legs' from red almond paste and anchor in position, using a little royal icing. Place 'all the King's horses, and all the King's men' in position round the base of the cake.

CHILD'S BIRTHDAY CAKE
Colour plate twenty

Use a round cake. Coat with almond paste and royal icing. Buy or make about 4 dozen pink sugar roses. Using a large star tube, outline the top edge of cake with shells. Place on a slightly larger round cake board, and finish bottom edge with shells. Arrange the sugar roses, about 1 in.

Humpty-Dumpty

Rocket Cake

Santa's Chimney

apart, round the top edge and base of cake, placing them alternately slightly above and slightly below the shell border. Cut a length of ribbon 1 in. longer than the circumference of the cake, fasten one end to side with a dab of icing, and when dry smooth ribbon firmly round sides of cake, turn in raw end and fasten in place with Sellotape. Place a group of pink sugar candle holders and candles in centre.

ROCKET CAKE
Colour plate thirty-two

Use a round cake. Coat with almond paste and blue royal icing. Make the 'mountains' on the moon with very stiff royal icing lifted up in 'peaks' on one side of the cake. Allow to set. Place ribbon in position round the cake, and ice the 'countdown' below it in deeper blue icing. Make 'moon men' from small, flat, round coloured sweets and angelica and hold in position with royal icing. Pipe faces with white royal icing, using a No. 1 or No. 2 writer tube. Finally place toy space men and rocket in position, flag on top of peak, holding in position with a little royal icing, if necessary.

SANTA'S CHIMNEY

You require: 1 pkt. chocolate finger biscuits • stiff icing, made from icing sugar and a little warm water (used as a cement to fix the biscuits together) • stiff card • Santa Claus ornament • cottonwool •

Cut a piece of stiff card approximately 4 inches square as a base. Fix four biscuits in a square so that one end of each finger overlaps the end of the next. On top of this fix another four, and continue for seven layers. Next cut another piece of card, 3½ inches square, and fix this across the top of chimney stack. Cut 6 more finger biscuits into halves and fix them on end in a circle to the card. Add a Santa Claus and cottonwool as illustrated to complete the decoration. As an extra surprise for the children the centre may be filled with sweets or chocolate.

All children will love this attractive centrepiece for their Christmas tea-table. Although the chimney is edible, rather than spoil the effect we suggest that the small guests be given instead tiny gifts

122

of sweets or chocolate from the chimneys' interior, with Santa's love, of course!

MERINGUE CHRISTMAS TREE

You require: For sandwich base: 6 eggs • 12 oz. butter • 12 oz. castor sugar • 12 oz. self-raising flour • For meringue: 3 egg whites • 6 oz. castor sugar • For butter cream icing: 2 egg yolks • 8 oz. butter • 16 oz. icing sugar • green colouring • vanilla • red colouring (carmine) • silver balls •

Cream butter and sugar until white and fluffy. Beat in the eggs and lightly fold in the flour. Divide the mixture between the following prepared sandwich tins: 7 in. sandwich tin, 6 in. sandwich tin and a 11 in. × 7 in. oblong baking tin. Bake at Mark 5, 375 deg., for 20-25 minutes, then leave to cool.

Make meringue: Place egg whites in a clean dry bowl and whisk until the whites stand up in points. Beat in half the sugar until the meringue is very stiff and then lightly fold in the other half. Place the meringue mixture into an icing bag with a plain vegetable pipe $\frac{3}{8}$ in. in diameter. Pipe on to a greased, greaseproof paper in small pointed domes about the size of a half-crown. Dry off in a very cool oven with the door slightly ajar, Mark $\frac{1}{2}$, 265 deg., for 5-6 hours.

Make icing: Beat the butter and sugar till stiff and creamy, then beat in the egg yolks with the vanilla flavouring. Take out two good table-spoons and colour bright red with the carmine colouring. Take out 1 teaspoon and leave uncoloured. Colour the rest of the butter icing green.

From the oblong sponge, cut circles of cake, using 5 in., 4 in., 3 in., 2 in., and 1 in. cutters. Using the 7 in. sponge as a base, form a pyramid out of the circles, begninings with the 6 in. sponge, sandwiching them together with a little green

Zodiac Cake

dry ingredients, mixing to a soft dropping consistency with a little warm water. Transfer the mixture into two 7 in. greased sandwich tins. Bake at Mark 5, 375 deg., for about 20 minutes. When cold fill with butter cream. Cover with white glacé icing and decorate as illustrated according to the age of the child, moulding hands of clock from almond paste.

ZODIAC CAKE

You require: For cake: 8 oz. butter or margarine • 8 oz. soft brown sugar • 1 tbsp. black treacle • 4 eggs • 12 oz. stoned raisins • 12 oz. sultanas • 8 oz. currants • 6 oz. glacé cherries • 2 oz. chopped almonds • 2 oz. mixed chopped candied peel • 4 oz. fine semolina • 6 oz. plain flour • 1 heaped tbsp. mixed spice • 2 tbsp. brandy or sherry • For almond paste: 8 oz. fine semolina • 8 oz. icing sugar, crushed and sifted • 8 oz. castor sugar • 2 egg yolks • ½ teasp. almond essence • ½ teasp. vanilla essence • 1 tbsp. sherry or milk • For royal icing: 3 egg whites • 1½ lb. icing sugar, sieved • 2-3 drops glycerine • cochineal •

Cream butter, sugar and treacle together. Beat eggs lightly and add slowly to mixture, beating well between each addition; this will keep the mixture stiff. Fold in fine semolina, sieved flour and spice. Fold in fruit and nuts. Lastly, stir in

butter icing, also coating the sides with butter icing. Stick the meringues in rows round the sides. Pipe the green butter icing in the spaces between the meringues, with a small star tube. Use the red butter icing to make holly berry clusters on the green butter icing. Place a small silver ball on the tip of each meringue using a little uncoloured butter icing to make it adhere.

CLOCK BIRTHDAY CAKE

You require: For cake: 4 oz. butter or margarine • 4 oz. castor sugar • 2 eggs • 3 oz. self-raising flour • 1 tbsp. cocoa • warm water to mix • For filling, icing and decorating: butter cream • white glacé icing • 12 chocolate buttons • 1 oz. almond paste, tinted red with food colouring •

Cream the butter and sugar until light and creamy. Gradually add the beaten eggs. Fold in the sieved

Clock Birthday Cake

liquid. Turn into an 8-10 in. cake tin, well greased, smoothing down mixture evenly. For the first half of the cooking time, cover the cake with two thicknesses of greaseproof paper. Bake in the centre of the oven at Mark 2, 310 deg. for 2 hours, and then lower to Mark 1, 290 deg. for a further $2\frac{1}{2}$ hours. The cake is baked when it is firm and elastic to touch and is shrunken slightly from the sides of the tin, and when a bright skewer, pierced into the centre, comes out undimmed. It is essential that the heat of the oven doesn't build up. If you find it hard to keep the temperature low, stand the cake on a board or extra thicknesses of paper on an oven tray during the last half of the cooking. Cool cake in the tin and leave paper on until ready to cover with almond paste and frosting. Make almond paste: Mix fine semolina, sifted icing sugar and castor sugar. Beat in egg yolks, essences and sherry or milk. Blend into a really smooth, pliable paste, taking care in the mixing that this is not wet. Roll out. Brush top and sides of cake with melted syrup or apricot jam. Cover neatly with almond paste and then wrap in aluminium foil or put into an airtight tin. Leave for 3 days for the almond paste to set really firmly. Make royal icing: Lightly whisk egg whites and then gradually add sufficient icing sugar to form a fairly stiff icing. Stir in glycerine then beat thoroughly till smooth and pure white.

Cover the cake with icing and quickly smooth sides and top with tip of a knife. When the icing has hardened, pipe white roses around the bottom. Into half the remaining icing, mix a few drops of cochineal until the icing is the colour you wish. The original cake was piped in bright red. There are 12 signs of the zodiac, so first pipe the divisions which make it easier for you to work in the signs neatly. When you have made the divisions, take a strip of red ribbon long enough to go round the cake. You can now see the divisions, so in white icing, pipe on to the ribbon the names of the signs of the zodiac in white. Carefully fix it in position.

Pipe the signs on to the cake; you can copy them from a magazine. Take a small lump of red icing and roll it out ready to make a star. Trace this from a piece of foil cut into a star shape and placed over the icing. Put in place, surround with dots.

Joy's Easter Nest

JOY'S EASTER NEST
Colour plate twenty-five

You require: For cake: 8 oz. self-raising flour • 8 oz. castor sugar • 8 oz. butter • 4 eggs • 2 rounded tbsp. desiccated coconut • For filling: 4 oz. butter • 6 oz. castor sugar • 1 teasp. vanilla essence • For decoration: 1 level tbsp. desiccated coconut • miniature chocolate Easter eggs • small yellow chick ornament •

Cream the butter and sugar together until light and fluffy, then beat in the eggs, one at a time. Fold in the flour and desiccated coconut gently with a metal spoon. Well grease a savarin mould, and fill with the mixture. Bake in a very moderate oven, Mark 3, 335 deg., for 45 minutes. Turn out carefully and cool on a wire tray. Sprinkle with the remaining coconut while the cake is still warm so that it will adhere. Place it on a serving dish. Make up the filling, and put into the centre of the cake. When quite set, mound up the foil-covered chocolate Easter eggs in the centre, and place the chick on top. (When serving the cake, remove eggs and ornament, and cut through to centre so that each person receives a portion of the filling with the cake.)

Many pretty variations can be achieved with this cake. The centre can be filled with flowers made from almond paste, tinted various pastel shades, and a handle fixed over the top made from angelica. Or a small circle of cardboard placed on the filling will support a tiny vase full of fresh flowers. But do not risk putting water in it!

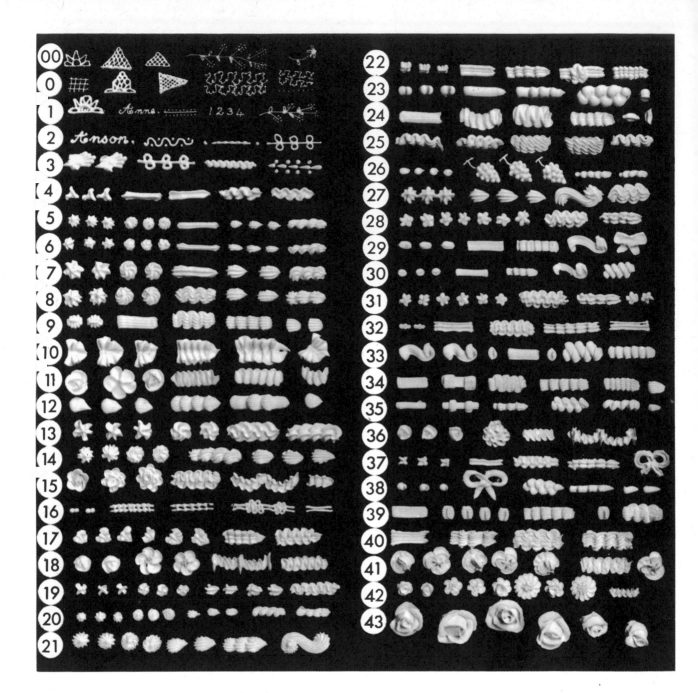

Demonstration chart of piping tubes

No.		No.		No.		No.	
00	Super Fine	11	Large Petal	23	Raised Band, wide	34	Ribbed Band, wide
0	Very Fine	12	Shell	24	Frilled Ribbon	35	Ribbed Band, narrow
1	Writer, Fine	13	5-Star	25	Upright Band, Fluted	36	Small Rose
2	Writer, Medium	14	10-Star			37	Fine Fancy Band
3	Writer, Thick	15	Dahlia	26	Grape	38	Raised Band, narrow
4	Small Border	16	Double Thread	27	Fancy Star	39	Fluted Ribbon
5	Rope	17	Small Leaf	28	Forget-me-not	40	Fluted Frilled Ribbon
6	Fine 6-Star	18	Large Rose	29	Ribbon, wide		
7	Large 6-Star	19	4-Star	30	Ribbon, narrow	41	Sweet Pea or Pansy Petal
8	8-Star	20	Fine Rope	31	Clematis		
9	Fancy Band	21	12-Star	32	3-Thread	42	Small Petal
10	Large Leaf	22	Border	33	Scroll	43	Super Rose

INDEX

Index continued